UP BY THE BOOTSTRAPS

Jorjan Jane

Author's Tranquility Press
ATLANTA, GEORGIA

Jorjan Jane/Author's Tranquility Press
3900 N Commerce Dr. Suite 300 #1255
Atlanta, GA 30344, USA
www.authorstranquilitypress.com

Ordering Information:
Quantity sales. Special discounts are available on quantity purchases by corporations, associations, and others. For details, contact the "Special Sales Department" at the address above.

Up By The Bootstraps/Jorjan Jane
Hardback: 978-1-964810-94-2
Paperback: 978-1-964810-95-9
eBook: 978-1-964810-25-6

Contents

DEDICATION

To Red, my dear husband,

I have written this book in honor and celebration of your life. You were never one to let any grass grow under your feet. You truly lived life to the fullest.

Love always, Sweet

PREFACE

The day Red was born, the trumpets sounded, the heavenly angels burst into song, and a voice from on high was heard saying, "LOOK OUT BELOW! Here comes Red, and you better be ready for him."

From the hills of the Kiamishi Mountains, in southeast Oklahoma, a boy picked himself up by the bootstraps, brushed off the Oklahoma dust and showed the world he was someone to reckon with. The only thing he knew was hard work. Deprived in more ways than one, he learned early in life to keep his mouth shut. But when he was on his own, he quickly made up for it, and never stopped after that. He became a mouth piece for all the cops in the state of Nevada, as well as nationwide. His grammar was less than perfect yet no one misunderstood what he was bluntly saying. He got his point across immediately and didn't mince words.

This is a remarkable story of a boy from the cotton fields to the oil fields, from trucker to pilot, from cop to labor leader, from lobbyist to senator. At one point he was either president or chairman of eleven different organizations at the same time. But his accomplishments didn't change him. As he always said, "I'm just a poor ol'country boy come to town trying to make good." And he certainly did.

This story shows that honesty, hard work, tenacity, and humor are still the best assets a person can possess. It opened doors which would normally have been slammed in his face, had he not had the foresight to stick his boot in the door ahead of time.

CHAPTER 1
Growing up in Oklahoma

Red came from a family of eleven, he being the youngest of the boys. They were an honest, hard-working family that lived on a farm in the poor back country of the Kiamichi Mountains of southeast Oklahoma. When he was growing up, the family grew cotton and peanuts but today I've heard the top crop is more lucrative. Pushmataha County is the marijuana capital. It is home to many thieves who are good for nothing welfare recipients as well as those on the lam.

His family was dirt poor without a pot to pee in, and I mean that literally because there was no inside bathroom. They didn't even have an outhouse. Now, that's poor! Everyone else in this Godforsaken land was practically in the same situation. The ground was overworked, and the post oak trees too scrubby and hard to cut. Red grew up in a four-room house with cracks in the wall so big that one could see outside. The wind would blow in cold damp air in the winter and hot humid air in the summer, along with the flies and mosquitoes. There was no electricity, and I will repeat, no plumbing. Need I say more?

Since he grew up with nothing, he appreciated all the little things most people take for granted. He never had a tooth brush. Instead, Red would peel back a twig from a tree to rub against his teeth to clean them.

The children wore hand-me-down shoes and only in the winter. The rest of the time they ran barefooted. Red may have been the youngest boy, but he was also the biggest, so he had a tough time wearing his brother's shoes. As a kid he was nicknamed "Tight Shoe." When he walked, he had an uncertain gait, as though there were pebbles between his toes from the ill-fitting shoes.

Forget about celebrating a holiday or even a birthday. It just didn't happen. He never got a birthday card, let alone a present, never a Christmas gift, nor was there a tree to decorate. The farm was surrounded by trees, but to cut one for Christmas was sheer foolishness according to his Dad. Every day was the same. Work was all he and his siblings knew.

He convinced his Dad that he could milk the cows, work in the field, and go to school, too, unlike his brothers, who didn't have the opportunity for schooling beyond the sixth grade. When the boys got out of grade school their formal education ended.

Three of the boys, including Red and one of the girls, stuttered badly. I feel it had something to do with their Dad's harshness. I never met Red's father but from what I have gathered, it was all work and no play. The kids were to be seen and not heard.

His father only had a second-grade education, but he could do math quickly in his head. Red would marvel at him at the auction barn. Red was great at math. He probably inherited that trait from his Dad.

I can only imagine the pressure of trying to raise a big family with the constant worry the crops could fail. If you don't have the money from the crops, what do you have left to fall back on?

His father traded off a wagon and horses for a truck. He never quite understood the workings of the new modern machinery. He would pull in a gas station and say, "Fill'er up and change the air in the tires."

At first the attendant said, "Change the air in the tires? Why would I do that?"

His dad responded, "Because the air gets stale, you know!" The one and only gas station in town became familiar with his Dad's request. The attendant would just fiddle with the valve stem, added a little air, then deflate what was put in.

His Dad wouldn't drive anywhere at night. "It burns up too much gasoline to run the headlights," he would say. Red could attest to that. He broke his arm one evening, and his Dad wouldn't drive him to town to the doctor until morning. By that time his arm was so swollen that it made it difficult to set.

His Mom worked in the fields along with the kids. Life was hard and showed on their sun toughened skin. Their fingers were cut and sore from pulling cotton balls. This was far from the sort of life anyone would envy.

His mother didn't have anything to speak of. His Dad made her hairpins from bailing wire. She made the kids' clothes from flour sacks. His Mom would cut old tire inner tubes to use as elastic in the waist of the girls panties.

He was raised on sausage, biscuits, and sorghum. Occasionally, he had chicken, squirrel, and possum with rice or beans. Not what I would call a big variety or even an appetizing one. "I never cared for possum," Red said, while grimacing. "It was much too greasy. And I wouldn't eat rice today if my life depended on it. Mom would buy it by the hundred-pound bag. I simply got tired of it."

Red never remembered getting a hug or a kiss or tucked in bed. It's amazing how someone who grew up with no affection could learn to be so attentive and loving.

He only remembers his angry father's short temper, the ranting, and then the silence. His Dad had a black bullwhip he used on the kids. Whenever they saw him angrily head to the barn they scattered, because they knew he was going for "the black snake" as his siblings referred to it. Red was the only one who dared to talk back or negotiate on behalf of his little sister, who wasn't allowed to go anywhere as a teenager without a chaperone—him.

CHAPTER 2
Jobs and Teen Years

Red's first job for wages was at the age twelve. It was at the one room school house where he arrived early to build a fire in the wood stove and warm up the place for the other kids. He would raise the flag, clean the blackboard and erasers, then sweep the floor after school.

Once a month, a man came to the school and setup a projector for the kids to view a movie. Red saved his money, so he and his little sister could go. It took all he had saved for the month, thirty cents.

Red remembered helping a neighbor catch pigs for castration. The farmer botched the job on one of the pigs and its insides fell out. The neighbor figured it was going to die so when Red asked if he could have it, the farmer said. "Sure, take it. Just understand that it isn't going to live." Red sewed it up, took it home, and hid it from his Dad. He fed it biscuits and, low and behold, the pig survived. When it weighed enough, Red took it to town and sold it. With the money, he bought a bike. It was shiny blue in color, the prettiest thing he had ever seen. That was his first taste of ownership. He liked the feeling.

Red had various jobs like cutting wood. The trees he cut were from his Dad's property. Red would not only cut it, deliver it, but stack it, as well, all for the grand total of fifty cents a cord. I am not talking about the times before World War II, I'm talking about the 1950's.

Before starting the ninth grade, Red and his buddy ran off to Texas with nothing but their cotton sacks to pick cotton. Their goal was to get enough money for a pair of brogan shoes and waist britches in order to start the new school year without wearing bib overalls and going barefooted. They slept under trees with the cotton sack as their pillow. Of course, they had no money for food, so the only thing they ate were apples picked from trees along the road.

High school was quite different from the one room school house. There were kids from town that made fun of country bumpkins. The city folks wore nice clothes, drove cars, and had money to eat lunch at school. On the other hand, Red carried a piece of cloth with a biscuit wrapped inside, and sometimes a piece of sausage, if there was any left from breakfast. He took a bus to school, but if there were any school functions like a dance or basketball game, he had to walk eighteen miles. For him, extra-curricular activities were few, because walking back home along the old country road and through the woods was difficult since it was pitch black. He liked the nights when the moon was full.

Joe, one of Red's brothers, bought him his first pair of cowboy boots. He loved them. They were maroon with a white eagle insert. Joe even bought shoe polish to match. It is hard to imagine Red as a young man without cowboy boots or western attire. That's all that I ever saw him wear.

Red had a brother, Art, who was shot up badly during the war. He spent three years in the Veterans' Hospital but his leg couldn't be saved. Red was a teenager when Art came home. He couldn't walk, so Red would carry Art on his back in the middle of the night, behind the barn to go to the bathroom.

Later Red had another brother who lost his leg. Red always felt so blessed even though he had health problems, he still had his limbs. He was thankful for that.

One brutally cold Saturday in December, Red was cutting wood for a neighbor, when he spotted a truck barreling down the dirt road leaving behind a trail of dust for half a mile. It was the preacher and Red's Dad. His father jumped out of the truck yelling, "You are going to marry the preacher's daughter for getting her pregnant!"

"Oh No, you have it all wrong," said Red. "I've never even held her hand!"

"You didn't hear what I said, boy. You are going to marry her!" bellowed his Dad.

The preacher piped up and added, "Next Sunday." Then he continued, "My daughter said you are the father, end of conversation! We will proceed with the marriage plans."

"No," insisted Red, but it fell on deaf ears. He knew her boyfriend, Roy, was a lazy, good for nothing, kid. They were in the same class at school. Red figured that Darla lied, because she knew her boyfriend's family all too well, and none of them worked. On the other hand, the Beal boys were hard working, responsible young men who could hold a job. Red was angry because she put the blame on him. She knew darn well who the father was.

Roy didn't step us to take responsibility and that also made Red mad.

Red was jarred into action. He felt he had no recourse but to run away rather than to get stuck marrying someone who was blaming him for her pregnancy. He really regretted not being able to finish high school and get his diploma.

Red's school mate Roy never fessed up to getting Darla pregnant, nor did he marry her but ironically, he dropped dead on the steps of the church one Sunday morning of a heart attack. He was just a young man. I guess the past caught up with him.

Red and his little sister kept in touch. She would tell him how things were going at home. His father didn't know where his son was. One day Red called his sister and she said, alarmingly, "Red, you got a draft notice and have to report to boot camp for army training!"

Off he went to the army but oh, he did not like it. He didn't like standing in line. "That's all you do in the army is stand in one line after another. There's never an end to it," he said, grumbling. "The army asked me what training I would like, so I told them truck mechanic. I figured I could put that to good use when I got out of the army and went back to driving trucks. They fixed me right up. I was assigned to work on track vehicles, tanks. Now how in the world am I going to use that knowledge when I get out of the service? *Track vehicles*, I kept saying to myself. *That's not practical.*"

He had the army take out a fifty-dollar allotment for his Mom from his sixty-five dollar a month pay. He was used to living on practically nothing.

When Red was on leave, he would hitch-hike home. It was quite a distance from Ft. Knox, Kentucky to Snow, Oklahoma. Naturally, it rained all the while he was trying to get a ride. All wet or not, drivers usually picked up hitchhikers in uniform.

His Dad was slowing down a bit, unable to keep up the pace and do what was necessary on the farm. Red, putting the past behind him, wanted to help out whenever he could. The Red Cross notified him at Fort Knox, "Your Dad is gravely ill. You need to return home." Red eventually got a hardship discharge from the army to help his Mom who was trying to run the farm by herself and take care of her husband, too. His Dad was soon taken to Wichita where there were big hospitals.

By now, all of Red's sisters and a brother were living in Wichita, and all but one worked at the Cudahy Meat Packing Company, a union packing house. Red had worked a few summers there as a teenager. He wasn't old enough, but he was big for his age and no one was the wiser.

Eventually, the farm was sold, and Red's mom moved to Wichita to be close to her husband and family.

When you live a meager existence with nothing but a roof over your head and some food, you appreciate what most people overlook. To this very day, Red marvels at a lit Christmas tree, gazing at it for hours. He loves ice and air conditioning. He's nuts over electronic gadgets, iPod, computers, DVDs, and TiVo even though he's not familiar with their use. Maybe that's why he has six TV's, seven refrigerator/freezers, and fifteen telephones in our home. He also has three cars, a high-end motor home, a golf cart even though he doesn't play golf, and an ATV (all-terrain vehicle). He has owned three airplanes, one with retractable gear. Then he had boats, the last one being a sixty-five-footer named the "Party Palace." I think that he believed the old saying that in the end, "He with the most toys wins." Red was trying to make up for all the things he didn't have as a kid.

CHAPTER 3
Bosses

Prior to the Army, Red worked for oil drilling companies. He started off as a roughneck (laborer) in Farmington, New Mexico. He worked his way up to a swamper (trucker's helper) then to a trucker, driving big rigs. He always raved about the man who taught him to drive. "He was the best! I was so fortunate to have someone who showed me the proper way to drive. He wouldn't tolerate any foolishness, and I understood I was there to learn all I could from him."

It was common practice, in the oil fields to have fifty hours of work under your belt by the middle of the week.

Red saved enough money to buy a car. Boy, he thought he was in high cotton!

Unfortunately, work slowed down so he found himself out of a job. He went northeast to Raton hoping to find work. He scoured the area willing to work anywhere. It had been a long, hot, humid day, and this was his last stop. He knew that he simply had to be hired, because he was not only hungry and thirsty, but his car was only running on gas fumes.

Red turned off a dirt road and flagged a trucker who just dumped a load of gravel.

"Where can I find the superintendent of this project?" he shouted over the noise of the loud diesel engine.

The driver pointed to the top of a hill and yelled, "The foreman's trailer is located on the south side of the hill." Red's car chugged up the grade. He found the boss speaking to a few of his employees.

"Howdy," Red said, as he put out his hand. "I'm looking for a job. What do you have for me?"

"Well," said the foreman, "What can you do?"

"I've been a roughneck, a swamper, and a trucker in the oil fields, but I'm willing to do just about anything," said Red.

"Can you drive heavy equipment?"

"Sure," said Red, with the most reassuring voice he could muster.

"See that bulldozer down on the plateau?" said the boss, in a raspy voice as he lit another cigarette.

"Yes sir," said Red, in his slow Oklahoma drawl.

"I want you to go down there and bring that piece of equipment up here."

"Okay," Red said. He headed down the hill, knowing damn well that he knew nothing about a bulldozer. His heart was thumping loud and hard, but his stomach was growling louder. He stepped up on the dozer and stared at the gears. He knew that he only had a few minutes to figure out how to drive it, and to get it up the knoll. He turned on the key and started pulling levers to get the bucket up. In a minute, he had the bucket in the air and was moving up the road. *That wasn't so bad after all*, he thought until he reached down to shift gears, and hit a lever that dropped the bucket. He pushed another lever, as his heart sunk down to his knees. He had just dug up the road in front of him and had a bucket full of dirt to prove it. Inadvertently, he kept digging up more of the road, until he pulled another lever, and started pivoting in a circle. He frantically pushed and pulled other levers, until the dirt dropped out of the bucket, but not on the road. More levers were pulled, as the dozer now rotated in the opposite direction. "Hell, what did I touch to do that?" He muttered to himself. Red was now sweating profusely. He needed to figure out the operating procedures, quickly. Fifteen minutes later he had filled in the road and was heading up the hill. When he rounded the curve, he spotted the boss and the same employees, holding their sides and laughing hysterically. The foreman said, "Hey, boy," as he gasped for air, "where did you learn to operate equipment?" Then he took another drag off his cigarette.

Red's face was solemn. He thought about not having enough gas to go anywhere else to look for work, if there was work to be had. His stomach was still growling and his mouth dry as a bone. The foreman drew in another short breath of air. "That's the funniest thing I've ever seen," he said, taking another drag off his cigarette. We need some humor around here and someone with determination. When can you start?" "Right now," Red said with a sigh of relief.

After six months the road project was complete, and Red was looking for work again. This time he had some more experience under his belt with operating various pieces of equipment. That was an asset.

Red went back to Farmington, New Mexico and hired on with a company that hauled oil rigging equipment. He was more familiar with that. The foreman was a real piece of work. He never had a nice word to say to anyone. He was always on the employees' asses for one thing or another. After several months, he assigned Red the task of taking a truck loaded with a heavy generator to the next work site located sixteen miles away. That site was in dire need of this piece of equipment.

"I can't do that, boss," Red said. "The generator is too tall. I would never make it through the bridge."

"Sure you will," Harlan said.

"No, there's simply not enough clearance."

"Did you hear what I told you to do, boy? Now get in that truck and get this over to the site. They are waiting for this generator."

"But…"

"There are no buts about it. I told you what to do. I hired you to work from the chin down, so do as I say. I'm the foreman and the brains of this outfit. I'm the only one that works from the chin up on this site and don't forget it!"

Red had been through that bridge quite a few times, and he had a good eye for judging heights and distance. He knew the truck would not fit. He tried once more to reason with the boss, which only infuriated the man more.

"You do it, or you are fired!"

So off Red went without another word. He looked over at his cohorts, but they just shook their heads. He was getting mixed messages. Did that mean they were siding with the boss? Did that mean he should just do as he was told? Or did that mean they also knew that he didn't have clearance?

He drove ten miles, then came to the steep downgrade that ended at the entrance to the old iron bridge. It had a faded worn sign "11 feet, 3 inches." He thought, *This is all or nothing*, as he down shifted. Nearing the bottom of the grade he changed gears, and this time it was full speed ahead. When he got to the bridge there was the most deafening sound of crunching metal and steel. Pieces of the generator were flying all over. The arch of the bridge, when first struck, bent, but the equipment he was hauling scattered everywhere. He didn't give a damn. He drove the remaining six miles and arrived at the site with little left of the generator. The shift superintendent uttered under his breath and barely audible, "What in the hell happened?"

"Well," Red said, "Harlan told me I had clearance for the bridge, and I begged to differ with him. He told me I was hired to work from the chin down, and, if I wanted my job, to just do as he said. So here I am just following orders," Red said, sarcastically.

The foreman blurted "Harlan is a son of a bitch. Thinks he knows it all. I'm calling him right now. Our work is temporarily shut down, until we get another generator. Hey kid, just drive the truck back to your work yard and tell Harlan he's an asshole. One of my employees will follow and bring you back here. I'll be needing an extra hand when we get a generator. You can work for me."

Red gladly took the truck back with the remnants of the generator still loaded. He thought how lucky he was to still have a job, and to now be working for someone decent. When he drove into the equipment yard, Harlan never looked up or said a single word. Anyone else who had a backbone would have been humbled by the mistake but not Harlan. He really was an asshole!

CHAPTER 4
Airline Flight

One weekend Red decided to fly back to Wichita to see his family. He went to the airport to get a ticket. Keep in mind that he had never flown before.

He asked what time the flight left, and the agent told him 1:15 p.m.

"When do I arrive?"

The agent said "1:25 p.m."

"Oh no, I've driven from Santa Fe to Wichita. I know how long it takes. I'll be damned if I'm going in something that only takes ten minutes to arrive. Forget about the ticket. I wanted to get there in a hurry, but not in a flash. I'll drive after all," he said, as he walked away.

The agent called out to him, "But sir, there's a time zone change." Red never heard a word the agent said because he was still baffled at how anything could go so fast. He just knew that ten minutes to go over five hundred miles was simply out of the question.

Red went back to New Mexico to work. One month later, after driving the truck into the work yard, his boss called him over to the side. "I just received a phone call from your sister. I'm sorry to tell you this but your father has passed away."

The superintendent gave Red an advance in pay, so he could fly home for the funeral. He didn't own a suit so his brother-in-law, who was larger than he, loaned him one. It was terribly big, but he was just grateful to have something decent to wear. He wore the suit with an old pair of beat-up work boots.

He wished he still had the cowboy boots his brother had bought for him, but he had worn them out a long time ago.

It was a solemn occasion with a positive outcome. He had the opportunity to see all his family again, and he had experienced his first airplane ride. That was a trill for him.

CHAPTER 5
Las Vegas

Red went to Grand Junction, Colorado to drive for Arapahoe Drilling Company and was tasked with the job of moving a huge piece of drilling equipment to the Nevada Test Site. When he saw the lights of Las Vegas that was all he needed to set his sights on moving and working there. "I drove down Fremont Street at night, yet it was as bright as day. I've never seen so many colorful lights in my life. I fell in love with Las Vegas. It was a town full of fun and energy."

He got a job at the Test Site driving trucks. He wanted to drive the double heavy-duty trucks, since he was used to driving big equipment. But it seemed the Mormons had that job classification tied up since it paid the most. The Mormons all tithed, so the more money the employee earned, the more the tithes to the church. Red later found out that the majority of city, county, and state government in Nevada was run by the Mormons. Unless you were one of them, you were out of luck.

I had arrived in Las Vegas from Lake Tahoe and was auditioning for shows on the strip as a dancer. I got a job right away, but I quit three days later when I was told, "Part of your job is to mix with the customers in between shows and after the show."

"No, I'm sorry that is not in my job description. I'm a dancer," I said, "not an escort."

The show producer who was a lecherous old man said, "Then look for work elsewhere. Goodbye." I had an inkling that I was going to have problems with him, when he told the dancers on the first day of rehearsals, "I want no boyfriends coming around the casino and no one can wear any engagement or wedding rings. Got it?" Then he would reach out to cop a feel. The very first day we learned to keep our distance. There were other shows for which to audition, so I moved on to greener pastures. Two weeks later I was working at the Desert Inn in "Hello America," a wholesome, patriotic show.

Red and I would pass each other on the apartment steps. He was heading to work, and I was just coming home. He was too shy to speak to me until we were properly introduced. He paid the landlord fifty dollars to introduce me to him.

I saw Red one evening sitting in the audience at the Desert Inn. I had just come out from a platform behind a high chandelier near the ceiling. As I came down the steps to the stage, I spotted him. He didn't recognize me at first. I was wearing a short black wig while doing a Gay Nineties number. I had on a low cut, red velvet costume that looked like a fancy corset and a large, sassy, red velvet hat with a white plume to the side, white gloves to my elbows and rhinestone necklace and earrings, fishnet stockings and red high heels. He innocently smiled, as if he liked what he saw. That bashful devil.

Our first date was a disaster. Red had asked me out, but I had turned him down because I already had a date. But that date didn't show up. Red had asked me to let him know if I reconsidered. I walked two apartments over and said, "I would like to go out with you after all, if the offer still stands." He grinned and said, "Yes." When I walked back to lock my apartment door, I noticed that the top nail had been removed from "number six" and it now looked like "number nine." I think there was a bit of conniving going on, but he never admitted it. Later I sat at the restaurant alone. Red ordered then spotted the teamster union boss in the parking lot and headed there to straighten out a problem. They had a big argument that almost came to blows. Red came back in, never ate a bite of his meal, paid the check, and we left.

The first time he invited me over to his apartment, he made it a point to open the curtains and leave the front door wide open. It was summer, and the air conditioner was on. I closed the door twice, but he opened it again. After we were married, I asked him why he did that. He explained that he was afraid of me. "I had money hidden in a sock in my underwear drawer, and I was fearful that you were going to take advantage of me, and somehow get to me for my money." *Oh, good heavens*! I almost hit him when he told me that.

He had been influenced by his mother's advice. She kept writing to him. "Come on home, son. These good ol' country girls are almost gone.

You won't find anyone decent in that sinful city where you are living. Hurry on home, now, ya hear?"

"He invited me to have breakfast with him in Los Angeles the following day.

"Sorry," I said, I wouldn't make it back to Las Vegas in time for work."

"Sure, you would. We'll fly down in the morning and be back by early afternoon."

"How are we going to do that, we haven't even made flight reservations?" I said. "We don't need reservations. I have my own plane."

That was a shocker! Here is this "poor ol' country boy come to town tryin' to make good" and he has his own plane and had a hangar in which to park it. I thought, *here is a guy who came from very humble beginnings and he has a plane. Wow! He is a go-getter. He is not going to let any grass grow under his feet.*

One day he said, "Why do you always take a cab to work when you have a Volkswagen in the apartment parking lot?"

"Well, I don't have a Nevada driver's license, no license plate for the car and I don't know how to drive a straight stick vehicle. I had the car delivered here, and that's where it has stayed."

He said, "I'm your man. I can help you." And that he did. I was so glad that he taught me to drive, because, in later years, he couldn't come back to me and say, "Who in the heck taught you how to drive?"

I was impressed with Red when he went to bat for me with the apartment manager, a young punk guy, who threw my clothes out of the wash machine. It had only been five minutes after the wash machine stopped, I went to the laundry room only to find my clothes on the floor, and the manager putting detergent in the washer with his clothes. When I told Red, he exploded. He had a spirited conversation with the young guy and it never happened again. I never had anyone stick up for me and I felt vindicated. This was a heart-warming experience to know that someone cared enough to fight my battles.

I was a single Mom with a three-year-old son. I felt honored that Red wanted to marry me and take on the extra responsibility of a child.

Two years prior, in 1962, my son, Gregory and I lived in Boston. He had been badly beaten by the babysitter's husband and wasn't expected to live. The Mormons came to the hospital every day to check on us. Gregory was only eight months old and had not been baptized yet. The Mormons blessed him, which made me feel a little more at ease. I figured that since Gregory was blessed as a Mormon, I should join the church and become familiar with their doctrine. When I left Boston, I headed to Harrah's Club at Lake Tahoe. The Mormon missionaries started coming around all the time. They were driving me crazy. I finally made a deal with them, and I joined the church at Mount Rose near Reno. I felt guilty about joining the church the way I did. It was really under protest. I was tired of them coming to my apartment door knocking so early in the morning, since I worked late at night. They were always offering to get me a job in a bank, but I loved dancing. They didn't think it was a savory environment. They also wanted to remove the coffee and alcohol from my apartment to avert any temptations. I had already quit drinking coffee and alcohol at the time, but I had friends that still drank, so I didn't want them to take it. I bulked. Finally, I said, "If I join the church will you promise to stop coming around and waking me in the morning or any other time of day?" The deal was made. They kept their promise, and I kept mine. I didn't go back to their church after being baptized, but I always kept their healthy doctrine in mind. Later, we resorted back to the Methodist church which was the religion I was raised in.

Red and I had a whirlwind romance and decided to get married on the weekend. On Thursday we went to city hall for our marriage license. At that time the fee was only two dollars. It was the day before Red got paid, and he only had one dollar. I pitched in a buck. I thought, *What's wrong with this picture?* I told him, jokingly, that I was marrying him for his money, but now I found out that he doesn't have any. Oh well, I was in for the long haul.

He said, "I'm no chauvinist. I'll let you pay half, that way you have vested rights. Isn't marriage a fifty-fifty partnership?" He was a quick thinker. I liked that trait.

We had a prenuptial agreement even before it was popular. We each had one stipulation. He could not get fat unless it was from a medical condition, and I couldn't cut my hair. That was it. I knew that he needed someone to cook for him, and he knew that I needed someone to be a father to Gregg. Our marriage license would be like a union contract, except it was for a lifetime, not to expire and renegotiate in two years.

Strange as it may sound, Red and I never celebrated our wedding anniversary on the same day. We went to the Little Chapel of the Flowers on February 13th. I swear that I said, "I do," at 11:58 p.m. He swears that he said, "I do" at 12:01 a.m., February 14th, Valentine's Day." I would not budge from my stance nor would he. So I always gave him his anniversary gift the day before Valentine's Day but he waited until the 14th to give me a box of candy and say "Happy Anniversary and Happy Valentine's Day." I always joked with him and said that he was just trying to get out of buying me a separate anniversary gift. Every year it was the same two-day celebration until we incorporated February 12th, Lincoln's birthday, to make it a three day holiday. That continued throughout the forty-nine years.

When Red went back to work at the Test Site on the Monday morning after we got married, he casually mentioned to his boss that he got hitched on Saturday.

"By the way, I married one of your kind, an LDS (Latter Day Saints) girl," he said, chuckling. The next day he was promoted to driving the double heavy-duty trucks. He came home from work elated saying that because I was LDS, he not only got promoted but would be receiving a nice pay raise as well.

"Just stick with me sweetheart and we'll go places," I said, smiling.

CHAPTER 6
Family

When I was expecting a child, Red was elated. Ultra sound was not yet popular, so we chose a boy's name and a girl's name, but no names for twins. Red's Mom was a twin, his Dad had twins in his family, and Red had twin brothers. Even though the evidence was likely I would have twins, I didn't feel I was carrying more than one baby. One thing I knew for sure, the child would be a soccer player as much as it kicked.

After our son was born, Red would hold him as if he were a fragile porcelain vase. He would look at his son, Travis, for the longest time with so much pride. I guess he was trying to figure out what this precious child was thinking. Fatherhood had such a positive and profound effect on Red, not to mention how good he treated his stepson Gregory.

When Travis was four months old, we flew to Wichita to meet his family. His Mom pulled him over to the side and asked, "Son, are you feeding your wife?"

"Yes," he replied.

"Well, it looks like she would blow away in a strong wind. I don't think she could do a day's work in the field."

"Mom, she is stronger than she looks," he said.

As I was speaking to his Mom, she stepped closer to me and reached up toward my cheek. I suddenly recalled Red telling me that one of the ways to tell a good horse is to look at his teeth. *Good Lord*, I thought, *she's going for my mouth*. But instead, she touched my face and said, "Soft, fair skin." I was relieved.

The family loved our new little red headed boy. I'm not sure they approved of Red marrying someone who already had a three-year-old son, but that was Red's decision he willingly made before we got married. He adopted Gregory before he started kindergarten. This way the whole family had the same last name. I was happy and contented. Life is good.

CHAPTER 7
Friend

Red had a friend named Derek, who he worked with in Farmington, New Mexico. Derek decided to come to Las Vegas to make better wages. He called Red to check out the prospects, and ended up moving here, and staying with us for eight months. He drove for a gasoline tanker company, and always came home smelling of fuel. I had to wash his clothes separately. I packed his lunch for him each day, as I did for Red, except Derek worked grave shift and slept during the day. Red worked dayshift, sleeping nights. Derek and Red were the best of buddies. Sometimes, when the weekends would roll around, they went out honky-tonking on a Saturday night to unwind from a busy work week. I had to stay home, because I didn't have a babysitter.

Their favorite spot was the Nashville Nevada Club. I had never been there, but I was told that each booth had a telephone. If you wanted to dance with someone at booth seven, then you dialed number seven and spoke with the person at that table. What a great way to break the ice.

"Hi, I'm Ray at booth three, if I mosey over to your table would you consider having the next dance with me?" Before anyone answered the question, they immediately looked over to see who they were talking to before accepting a dance. Sometimes there was a little wave or a "howdy Ma'am," and a tip of the cowboy hat. One of Red's other hangouts was the Lariat Club on Western Avenue.

I was familiar with the Lariat. I recalled when we first went there on a date. We got a table and ordered a drink. Red was a Jack Daniels man. I would think of John Wayne swaggering up to a bar, slamming his hand down with a few coins and saying,

"WHISKEY." I think Red was trying to get up enough nerve to ask me to dance. He finally stood up, held out his hand and said, "Would you like to shine my belt buckle?" I gave him a blank look until he nodded toward the dance floor. He only liked to slow dance. I would get so tickled because he would never talk to me when we danced. I would ask him a question but he wouldn't answer. When the song was over I would ask the question again and found out that he was too busy counting the beats to the music. Red didn't want to get confused. "I was afraid of screwing up, if I took my mind off the song," he would say so seriously.

Red had an unusual habit of sleeping with at least one eye open and often both. When we first got married, I found it unnerving. It seemed that when I got up in the night, he was watching every move I made. Eventually, I got used to it.

It nearly scared Derek to death when he first saw this. Derek rode with Red on a truck run to California. Derek offered to drive part of the way. When they switched places, Red went right to sleep. He was a heavy sleeper. Derek said something to him, and Red didn't answer. He looked over at Red, and both of his eyes were open. Derek repeated, "Red, do you want to stop for coffee?" There was still no movement. He shook Red's arm but no response. Derek thought he had died. He pulled over quickly and shook Red as hard as he could.

Red jerked up quickly and said, "What's the matter?"

"I thought you were dead!" shouted Derek, nervously. Why do you sleep with your damn eyes open?"

"I'm watching the snake with one eye and looking for a stick to kill it with the other one," said Red.

His friend Derek went to Colorado to drive logging trucks. One tragic day, he was going down Wolf Creek Pass and lost the brakes on the truck. He flipped it going seventy miles an hour and was crushed to death by the truck and the logs. His brother called Red and said that every bone in his body was broken. Derek was only twenty-six years old.

Red had just started a new job, so he humbly asked the boss for a few days off to fly back to the funeral. The boss reluctantly gave him Friday off. His employer flatly stated, "If you aren't back by Monday morning, consider yourself fired." Red had borrowed money for an airline ticket to fly back for the funeral on Saturday. Derek's body hadn't been transported back to Grand Junction so Red stayed until

Sunday night. The body still hadn't arrived. Red flew home in time to go to work on Monday without being able to say goodbye to his best friend, Derek. He was so disheartened. Besides having to pay back the borrowed money, he had returned without going to Derek's funeral. It all seemed so sad and futile.

CHAPTER 8
Trucker's and Their Lingo

There were layoffs at the Test Site, but Red was never without a job. Sometimes the new job didn't pay well but it was work and a paycheck. Once he called someone he used to work for in Durango, Colorado, and drove back for several months until the strike was settled at the Test Site. There were more strikes and more layoffs at the test site, so Red hired on as a truck driver with the Safeway grocery chain, round-tripping California each day. He sat in on contract negotiations for the teamsters with the grocery chain and got a real education on how big corporations' work. That was an eye opener to him.

When we would get together with Red's truck driving friends, I was lost in their conversation. They talked about Jake a lot, so I thought he was one of their buddies. Well, actually Jake was a real important buddy. I found out that they were talking about the invaluable jake brake on a truck. I also thought Jimmy was a friend, but that was a GMC truck. Go figure. I was confused when they referred to the "peter belt." I thought it was a jock strap for truckers when actually it was the brand name of a truck called a "Peterbilt." Oh boy, did I have a lot to learn. I wrote to the National Truckers Association for a handbook on trucker's language and terminology.

Several years later, Red worked for Dean's Roofing Company, hauling roofing materials from southern California to Las Vegas. One hot August day, when Red was hauling tar paper for the roofing company, his load started shifting. The tar paper was stacked and tied securely, but, with the intense heat, it was going limp. The top rolls were sinking into the layer below causing it to become too flimsy to stay upright. The load kept swaying from side to side. Cautiously, he made it to Las Vegas without incident. If Red had his druthers, his ideal load would be hauling canaries. "All you need is a kid with a stick to wave it around and keep the birds flying," he would say with a smile. "Not a heavy load at all, and I wouldn't have to struggle getting the rig up Baker's grade or Cajon Pass, which is eighteen miles of hard climbing."

I rode with him once but never again. Good heavens, what a bumpy ride! I was so sore. I thought my kidneys were going to be jarred loose. Guess I wasn't cut out to be a trucker.

Some of the conversations from the CBers were weird. Others were crude even though the FCC forbids foul language. The CB radio was handy, if there was a wreck ten miles down the road. Truckers would advise other drivers to get over in the hammer (fast) lane. If there was debris, they would advise of a mattress in the road at mile marker twenty two. But mostly you heard, "Hey good buddies, there's a smoky south of the underpass and a bear in the air. Must be hunting season."

"Anybody got your ears on? This is Pistol Packing Mama. There's a Pavement Princess at the next truck stop if any of you fellas are horny."

"Hey Six Pack, put the petal to the metal 'cause we got a convoy. I know you just stopped for some road tar (coffee), so now you should be able to make it from L.A. to New York, non-stop. Step it up."

I bought a CB hand book to understand what the truckers were saying because I didn't have a clue. They don't teach that in college.

CHAPTER 9
Flying

Red wanted to utilize his VA loan by taking more flying lessons. He eventually got his instrument ratings and multi-engine ratings. He built his hours by flying for Mustang Airlines, a small operation. He would pick up the prostitutes from the nearby brothels in Lida Junction, Latrop Wells, and Beatty and bring them to Las Vegas for their regular check-ups at the County Health Department. All the while, he was building more flying hours. While flying, he often repeated to himself, "Lose not thine airspeed lest the earth rise up and smite thee." It was like a mission statement for the pilots. I smiled whenever I heard the saying. I found it quite appropriate.

Red met a man at the airport who was well respected and had owned several planes. He had a plethora of flying experiences. Brad was also knowledgeable about most airplanes. Red loved to pick his brain. He was old enough to be Red's father. I figured Brad to be in his sixties. They really hit it off as friends. We had been invited to his home for dinner several times. His wife was a CPA for a big corporation. She also offered to prepare our IRS taxes for a couple of years.

One day Brad asked Red if he would be interested in renting our plane to him. "Sure," said Red, knowing that he couldn't find anyone more qualified. Before the deal was consummated, Brad asked "Would you be interested in building more flying hours?"

"Yes," said Red. "I'm listening"

Brad said, "I often fly to Chihuahua, Mexico to a Catholic Mission to deliver bandages, aspirins, and first aid supplies. Would you like to fly there tomorrow?"

"I'd like that," Red said, with anticipation. I was happy for Red to get this opportunity. Brad brought his maps for Red to look over. They would be flying in our plane into the Sierra Madras by Copper Canyon.

There was a small dirt landing field near a village inhabited by the Tarahumara Indians. Red was fascinated by this culture. He watched the Indian men kicking big rocks, barefooted. He cringed thinking how hard that was on their toes, but they never flinched. They also ran long distances in a dead run. He was amazed at their ability and endurance. He watched mothers putting their unclothed babies in a rope swing harness tied to a tree about five feet off the ground, so the goats and chickens wouldn't harm them. I guess that eliminated the need for diapers or laundry. Red and Brad slept outside like everyone else, except they were the guests, so they didn't have to sleep on the ground. They got a cot. The bugs and mosquitos were a nuisance. Red was awakened by a terrible squealing sound. He jumped up only to find that a pig was stuck underneath his cot. Brad thought that was real funny, but Red didn't. It had startled him.

Red had built up a lot of flying hours and was ready to put in applications for the airlines. Flying was his passion. I always thought, *I wouldn't want to give Red the choice between flying or me.* I think he would have chosen flying. But on the other hand, I loved dancing, that was my passion.

Red was hired by Apache Airlines, but the domicile was Phoenix. He had to move there, get an apartment, and fly home on the weekends. This airline had low pay and offered no benefits. But the boys and I saw him more when he was a pilot than when he was driving a truck from six in the morning to midnight.

When he was a trucker, I had mentioned to him, "One day, honey, you are going to turn around, your boys will be all grown, and you won't even know who they are. Please cut back on your hours and I will go to work to help out." This new job as a pilot provided Red with a little more time at home and that was great.

Red recalled flying into Minot, North Dakota one cold winter day. The heater in the plane didn't work. There was a little old lady shivering so much her lips quivered. After landing, he helped her out of the aircraft and into the warm terminal. "This is uncalled for," said Red, as he filed a complaint with his supervisor. The maintenance records for the fleet of aircraft were deplorable.

Later, Red was trying to land in Billings, Montana, but he had to do so by instruments alone. It had snowed all morning, and he couldn't see out the window to taxi to the gate. The windshield wipers were broken. He had to open the window and reach out as far as he could to scoot the snow off the windshield. How ridiculous is that?

Red grounded the plane in Billings and said, "Unless the plane is up to par, I am not going to fly it to the next stop in Helena, Montana. His supervisor said, "You can't ground the plane!" Red said, "Watch me!" He had no fear of going straight to the top with his complaint. He refused to fly and there was not another pilot to take over. Red called the owner in New York and explained the situation. "I love to fly, but there are too many maintenance problems that aren't addressed. If the plane crashes due to lack of proper maintenance, then I have defeated my purpose, and you will lose your airline." The conversation fell on deaf ears.

Red simply could no longer work for someone who put money ahead of safety and people's lives. He gave a two-week notice. Three weeks later, one of the planes crashed near Tucson, killing all the passengers, the pilot and co-pilot. Red's two co-workers had refused to complain about the maintenance, and it cost them their lives. The airline was sued so the owner filed bankruptcy.

Red owned three different airplanes over the early years of our marriage. His favorite was the orange and cream-colored Mooney Executive with retractable gear and low wings. Whatever Red saw and wanted, he worked more hours to get it.

CHAPTER 10
Mazatlan

We had been married for five years and still hadn't taken a honeymoon. There were two reasons for that. First, we had very little money when we got married and what we had was allocated for bills. Secondly, my stepdad died, unexpected, the day we were to be married. It was not a joyful time.

Five years had passed. Mom offered to watch the boys while we took our honeymoon to Mexico, if we brought the kids to Arizona. We flew there in our Cessna, dropped the boys off, then flew to Mazatlan, Mexico.

Prior to our trip Red had asked me to learn some Spanish, in case we needed to understand what the control tower was saying. I took a six-week, conversational Spanish class, but it didn't help. Upon circling the airport in

Mazatlan, Red said, "What did the tower just say to me?"

"I don't know honey, maybe they will repeat it."

"Whiskey 5472, Control."

"Red, all I understand is our tail number. I can't even tell if they are speaking broken English or Spanish."

Red finally circled the tower and saw a controller point to the runway in front of us. "This is embarrassing," Red said, as he landed. It was nearly dark, and we knew we couldn't land at night, because the airport had no runway lights. It was already dusk. We were literally flying by the seat of our pants, tempting fate.

The private airport didn't have any tie downs. We had to rig a rope and some concrete blocks to hold the plane in place. We prayed that no wind would come up. Shortly after landing, several young boys came running up to us. One said, "I'll stay here and watch your plane, Mister, for two dollars a day." The other kid was saying the same thing, only louder, trying to drown out the voice of the first boy, who I assumed was his brother. We chose the older one. He was about twelve.

"Deal." said Red, shaking his hand. A week later the kid was still there. He must have gone home to eat and sleep, but we didn't know for sure.

Maybe he and his brother took turns.

We went downtown shopping on the second day of our stay in Mazatlan. It was nearly noon, and the sun was hot and glaring. Red had just bought a new pair of sun glasses that folded in half and fit easily into his shirt pocket. Now he needed a straw hat, since his baseball cap didn't protect his ears from the piercing rays.

"Hey Lady, over here, look. I give you special deal. Look lady, I have good stuff. Buy from me."

"No," I said shaking my head and pointing to the hat I had just bought. "You buy something to take home for your kids." "No," I said assertively and continued walking.

"Hey Mister," beckoned a beautiful girl with big brown eyes. "You buy from me, I have what you want," she said in a sultry voice. "You want a hat? I sell good hats." She caught him by the arm before he could walk away. "Look," she said, "I sell special hat." She took the hat off her head and squashed it flat between her hands, then shook it back to its original shape. Then she folded it and put it in his back pants pocket, pulling it out quickly saying, "Hat carries easy, packs easy." I watched closely making sure she didn't remove his wallet. Red was amazed that the hat was so soft and pliable. It was definitely a good hat.

"I give you special price, my friend," she said in a whisper.

"How much?" said Red.

"For you, only twenty-five dollars," said the pretty girl, flirting and batting her eyes.

"No." Red said, "Too much!"

"How many you want? Two, three, four? I make you special price." "One," said Red as he held up his index finger. "Okay Mister, I give to you for twenty dollars." "No deal," he said and turned away.

"Okay my friend how much you pay?"

"Five bucks," said Red, holding up his left hand with five fingers spread.

She looked at his wedding ring and said, "You a rich hombre but me, I am poor and have three kids to feed." There was a long pause as she pouted then said, "fifteen dollars." "Six dollars," said Red.

"Ten dollars, she retorted, "so I can buy milk for my kids."

"Six dollars or I'll buy the hat from someone else." He turned and walked down the street.

"Ten dollars," she shouted as he continued to walk. There was no response from Red.

"Okay Mister, six dollars," she yelled as she caught up with him and held out her hand for the money. When paid, she put the hat on his head.

"I don't make any money today," she said in a pathetically dejected tone.

Red was happy to have his new hat and at the price he negotiated for. I only paid three dollars for my straw hat, but it was tacky looking. Red said that I looked like a field hand.

"Oh well, it shades my face from the sun, and I will only be wearing it for a week, leaving it behind in the hotel room when we head home. It will have served its purpose." "Hungry?" Red asked.

"Not much," I answered.

"Well, I could eat a side of beef, since I worked up an appetite on that negotiation." We stopped at a taco stand on the corner, a one-man operation. I was too squeamish to order after assessing the cleanliness of his cart. There were flies everywhere, some sitting on the meat cooking on the grill. I waved my hand to shoo them away, but to no avail. They didn't budge. The vender picked up a can of bug spray and proceeded to fill the air with a putrid smell as I watched the spray drift down onto the meat.

"That's it Red, I'm not eating anything." My eyes were still wide open in a state of disbelief. "I'll wait until we get back to the hotel to eat." Red ordered three tacos and a side of refried beans that looked disgustingly similar to something a dog would leave along the side of the road. He thought it was all delicious but of course, he had a cast iron stomach, nothing he ate made him sick. I'm the queasy one. I shuttered to think of him drinking filthy creek water as a kid in Oklahoma, but he did. His immune system must have been terrific. As for me, I'd be dead.

When we arrived back at the hotel lobby, we were greeted by our new friends from Grants, New Mexico, whom we had met the night before.

They were both school teachers, and interesting to speak to.

"Been shopping?" they asked.

"Yes," Red said, excited to show them his purchase. He took off his hat, which made him look like Jimmy Buffet in Margarita Ville.

Red began, "See how practical this hat is. It can fold up and fit in your pocket and it's easy to pack." He began to demonstrate its pliability, smashing it together in his hands. There was a crunching sound. He shook it so it would return to its original shape, but there was only loose straw between his fingers. Most of it fell on the lobby floor. There was nothing left in his hands that resembled a hat. He stood there with his mouth open, and a blank look on his face.

"She must have switched hats!" he said in disbelief. "I've been had!" Our friends smiled politely but not me. I was roaring and holding my sides.

Here Honey, I blurted, you can have my hat. It's your turn to look like a field hand.

The nice couple wanted to show us their favorite scenic spot in Mazatlan. "Meet us in the lobby at eight this evening, and we'll take you there." We agreed.

The drive was only a few miles from the hotel. We arrived at this concrete staircase jutting out into the water. At the top was a tower platform with a railing. Gail said, "Here is what we do. As the tide goes out you count the seconds. If you run fast enough, you can get to the top without being washed off the steps into the ocean. It's a wonderful view from the top."

"Maybe so," I said," but if you slip you are washed out to sea, and if you survive the fall onto the jagged rocks below, you are broken to bits. No thank you."

"Oh, come on! We have done it many times. It's all a matter of timing."

"Okay," Red said, "let's go." I looked at him strangely, thinking that must have been the Margaritas talking. "I think it's a crazy and dangerous idea." "You aren't going with us?" Gary said.

"No, it's insane."

"Guess you aren't up to the challenge," he snickered. "Don't you want to experience something different? You're on vacation. Live a little."

"Yes, that's what I want to do live, live a little longer."

My birth sign is Aries and I never back down from anything, so the problem arose when Gary started goading me into doing it.

"Take the challenge. What are you afraid of? Remember, nothing ventured-nothing gained."

"Okay," I finally said, reluctantly.

The tide came in and we stood ready to run. Gail said, "Remember, we only have forty-five seconds to get to the top where we will be safe. As the tide started to recede, she yelled, "Go, one, two, three, four, five." Gail and

Gary was first and second, Red was third in line, and I was the last. The teachers were wearing jeans and gym shoes. Red had on slacks and cowboy boots. As for me, I was inappropriately dressed for such a fete. I had on a pink shirtwaist dress, stockings, and pink sling heels. I made it to the steps which were about two feet wide. There were probably twenty-five steps in all with no railing. I kept slipping on the moss.

"Oh heavens, what's pinching my legs so badly?" I looked down and saw crabs hanging on my stockings and digging into my skin. This was freaking me out. I pulled off my shoes, but my stockings were just as slippery on the wet steps as the leather soles. I wondered how Red was managing in his leather cowboy boots. Evidently, better than I. He was about five steps ahead. I looked like an infant, on all fours, with my butt in the air, now crawling up the steps, so I wouldn't fall off the side into the rugged rocks below. I could hear Gail yelling, "thirty-nine, forty, forty-one."

"Oh Lord, this is not how I imagined my death. I don't want to be swept out to sea from some scatterbrained idea. If I survive, I'll never go along with the crowd again. Lord, I swear, I will never-ever do such an idiotic thing."

"Forty-two, forty-three, forty-four." I saw Red's hand reach down to pull me up the last two steps to the platform, just as the waves came barreling through. As I stood at the top, shaking badly, I remember saying, "Where's the spectacular view? I see nothing." It was quite dark, that is why I didn't see all the moss on the steps or the wicked crustaceans.

Oh, dear God, I'm at the top now, but how am I going to get down? The downward decent is going to be worse. If I slip, who will raise the boys?

Gail and Gary headed back down as the tide started to recede. One, two, three, four. I waited a few cycles of the tide, not sure how I was going to handle the decent into hell. I took off my stockings with the crabs still hanging on. I left my shoes behind, because if I fell, I wouldn't need them anymore. I sat down on my butt at the top steps and went bump, bump, bump all the way down. My dress was soaked and stained from the green moss. My tailbone was sore, because I was sitting on crabs each step down, but I made it with five seconds to spare.

I couldn't believe that Red was game for such a stunt. I think he regretted the challenge, too. After all we were adults with two young sons to raise. How foolish was that! I blamed alcohol for clouding our judgment. We have done some stupid things in our lives, but that topped them all. Ever since that night, if something doesn't seem right, then I won't do it. Period!

I never went along with the crowd after that incident. And I rarely have no more than one drink unless I'm at home.

It's like police work. If you make a dumb mistake and are lucky enough to live to tell about it, you won't ever make that same mistake again.

Experience is such a good teacher.

CHAPTER 11
Police officers

Every Sunday we would sit at the donut shop, have coffee, and talk about our future. It sounds funny now, having coffee and donuts before we were ever cops. Red said, "We need to work for a county, city or state entity so we can have retirement benefits. They also have sick leave benefits and vacation leave. If we are going to look toward the future, that's what we need to do." I cringed thinking that I would have to work somewhere for twenty years. I get bored too easily. It would have to always be a challenging job.

Red and I put applications in at the County Fire Department, the City Police Department and the County Sheriff's Department. He was called first by the city police, so he hired on with them. Two months later, I got a call from the Sheriff's Department and went to work as a meter maid at McCarran Airport.

I've always heard in order to get a job, it's who you know, not what you know. Well, that wasn't the case for Red and me. Or at least, I didn't think it was. While waiting for my interview at the Sheriff's Department, the secretary kept looking at me and finally asked, "Who is your husband?" After telling her, she got such a serious look on her face. I thought she was going to cry.

I passed the interview with flying colors, although I had no previous experience. I remembered the secretary's name, so when I got home, I asked Red if he recognized her name. "Oh yes," he explained, "her ex-husband use to work at the test site with me. He was a heavy drinker. She called me on Thanksgiving Day about six years ago and asked me if I would go looking for him. She seemed very concerned. I agreed to search.

"You remember, Sweet, that was our first Thanksgiving we were going to spend together but I never showed up in time to eat."

"Oh yes, I certainly remember that day." I was hotter than a jalapeno.

Red continued, "I drove along Boulder Highway and looked in the parking lots of numerous bars. I also checked the motels along the way thinking I would find him sleeping off a bender. I spotted his car at a rundown motel, and knocked on the door of the room that was in front of his parked car. There was no answer. I tried the doorknob, and the door was unlocked. I opened it just enough to see Chuck sitting on the bed with a gun to his head. I walked in slowly and asked him if I could have a drink with him, since I saw a bottle of whiskey sitting on the nightstand. I asked him to put the gun down, so we could talk for a few minutes. He was distraught over his divorce and was going to end his life. I talked him out of it and told him I would drive him home. Later, I called his ex-wife and told her what had happened. She couldn't thank me enough. After all Chuck was the father of her son."

"Honey, why didn't you tell me that story on Thanksgiving when you missed the big dinner I had fixed. I was angry with you for not calling me to let me know you wouldn't be there. You finally showed up four hours later with no explanation and three sheets to the wind. I would have understood if you told me what had transpired. You could have confided in me, but, no, you are the big silent type," I said, shaking my head, and giving him a kiss to let him know I loved him anyway. He would never discuss emotional issues.

I worked my way up the ladder, having passed all the tests and completing the police academy. The city and the county law enforcement merged. I was one of the first three women hired by Metro to be a patrol officer. Now, Red and I would be working for the same department. There was a nepotism rule. No relative could work in the same department, but since he originally worked for the city, and I had begun with the county, I was grandfathered in.

The government had given the police department a grant to hire minorities, which they did, except for women. They were still discriminating. When the government threatened to take back the money already allotted, Metro was in a jam, so they hired their first females. Originally, the dispatchers attended the police academy. Two were transferred to the patrol division along with me from the airport.

Red and I would relay war stories to each other after our shifts. Red was glad to be working for the police department, where he had some decent benefits, compared to truck driving and flying for a non-union airline.

I met some of the guys on his squad. I sure didn't like one of his lieutenants. He was so arrogant. He thought he was being cute by saying that he was going to put Red on a "word a day" program, so he could learn to talk better. He assigned Red to the black area of town, because he said that Red didn't know how to communicate with educated people. How on earth did this lieutenant move up the ranks with an attitude like that?

Red flourished in the black area, graveyard shift. He knew everyone including their mammas and their aunties. Sometimes the teenagers would get smart with Red, and bring up the fact that he was just harassing them because they were black or poor. He said, "I worked in the fields in Oklahoma from morning to night, picked cotton, which you probably never did, and had to run barefooted, because I didn't own a pair of shoes that fit. I ate possum when you probably had nice meals, or the opportunity to go to a restaurant. I never had a coke, hamburger or French fries. You probably got a decent haircut, rather than have a bowl put on your head, and the rest shaved off around it. I never saw a TV or had air conditioning. Didn't even have electricity. "Now, tell me, if that's not poor and disadvantaged, then I don't know what is. Did you go through that?" he would ask.

"No sir," they answered respectfully.

One night Red was sent on a disturbance call. The dispatchers were familiar with Ms. Johnson and her reoccurring complaint. Not Red, he was still a rookie.

"I Delta 2, Control, respond to 478 McWilliams Street, see Ms. Johnson reference home invasion."

"1 Delta 2 responding."

When Red arrived, he saw an elderly black woman waiting on the porch in her nightgown, and a blanket thrown around her shoulders. She shouted,

"They be in the house again!" "Who?" said Red.

"Same ones," said Ms. Johnson.

"Do you know who they are?" Red inquired.

"Sur nuff do. The haints be in there."

"Excuse me Ma'am, who did you say was in there?"

"The haints," she repeated loudly. "I ain't able to sleep. I don't wants them in there no mo."

"How many are there?" asked Red.

"Must be six or mo."

"Ms. Johnson, are haints like ghosts?"

"Sur nuff," she said, as she shivered and shook her head in dismay.

Red thought for a minute then asked her if she had any bleach.

"Yes, sir." She pointed to the open door and said, "It's under the sink," not wanting to go inside.

"Come on Ms. Johnson, walk with me, and we'll get it"

She was hesitant, but slowly proceeded into the house as close to Red as humanly possible. When the bleach was retrieved they headed outside again, Ms. Johnson right on Red's heels. Red poured a stream of bleach across the walkway by the front gate. He then handed the bottle to Ms. Johnson to hold. Red removed his hat and ran, swinging it inside the house from room to room, yelling, "Get out of here, Get out, you hear me. Shoo, shoo!" he shouted as he swung his arms, as if swatting at a swarm of bees. He got to the back of the house, and called Ms. Johnson to meet him at the back door. She swiftly complied but was curious at this spectacle.

"Ma'am now hand me the bleach again," he said, breathless from all the exertion. Ms. Johnson watched him pour more bleach along the back fence line.

"It's all done," said Red. "The haints won't cross over the bleach at the front gate, and since I've chased all of them out of the back door, they won't come back in. You won't have any more problems with them. Good night."

"Wait a minute officer," said Ms. Johnson. "I be havin' this problem for twenty year and no po-liceman ever did that for me. I can't thank you enough. I'm going to bake you a pie. Stop by tomorrow night during your shift and pick it up."

"Thank you, Ma'am, but that's not necessary. I'm just doing my job."

"Control, 1 Delta 2, problem resolved."

Three months had passed and no more calls from Ms. Johnson. Dispatch was amazed. One evening at briefing, the sergeant asked everyone to remain seated until he read a letter mailed to the Sheriff.

Dear Sheriff,

My name is Ms. Johnson and I be livin' at 478 McWilliams Street.

At this point Red knew what was coming and he slumped down in his seat. *Oh, Lord, I'll never live this down. I'll be the laughing stock of graveyard shift.* The sergeant continued reading.

Three months ago, a policeman was sent to my house to get rid of the haints, cause they be coming in all the time, disturbin' my sleep. I don't be knowin' the kind officer's name, but he had red hair. I want to thank him for ridding the haints from my house forever. He poured bleach at my gate and shooed them out through the back door. Then poured more bleach to keep them from coming back in. I never seen anythin' like it, but it sur nuff worked.

Yours truly,

Ms. Mabel Johnson

By now the squad was rolling on the floor with laughter. Red thought he couldn't be lucky enough to get a commendation from one of his good busts like catching a murder suspect. Oh, no, now he figured he would be stuck working every Halloween and nights when there was a full moon. His fellow officers started calling him "The Ghost Buster."

Red liked to hear about some of the different stuff that happened on my shift.

While I was on patrol, I was dispatched to the Boulevard Mall security office to transport a black female shoplifter to jail. After getting the paperwork, I headed back to the patrol car. A chunky five-year-old boy ran up to me excitedly and wrapped both of his legs around one of mine. I nearly lost my balance because I had my right arm interlocked with the handcuffed prisoner, and she was jerking back and forth, not being cooperative.

The little boy screeched, "Are you on the squat team?"

"No," I said, "I'm not on the swat team. Now go back to your mother." "No, I'm going with you," he said bluntly.

I tried taking a few more steps dragging the boy along. *This is ridiculous*, I thought. *I'm limping straight legged like Chester in the western series of Gunsmoke. This would be a perfect time for the suspect to run.*

I called to the boy's mother, "Mom, get your son."

She just laughed. "He loves cops."

"Evidently," I said, "but he needs to be with you." "Can I play with your gun?" blurted the snot-nosed kid.

"No!" Go to your Mom."

I was trying to keep my elbow snug to my side, so he wouldn't unsnap the holster. I turned around and yelled, "Ma'am, get your son, right now. This isn't cute."

"I think it is," she smirked. "Take him to jail."

"Yea," the kid repeated, "Take me to jail! Put the handcuffs on me! Call out the squat team!"

I started kicking my left leg hoping to knock him off, but he held on with a death grip. Then I realized just how excited he was when he started humping my leg. *Good grief, is this a kid or a dog?* I thought. As I approached a fire plug, I swung my leg against it hoping to squeeze him hard enough, so he'd let go but he was like a fluffy pillow. It didn't phase him. *There is no way that I can book a five-year-old for interference, but I'd sure like to.* I finally made it to the patrol car, placed the suspect inside, and put the seat belt around her. I yanked that kid from my leg, drug him to his mother, seething, and said, "Don't ever let this happen again. If my suspect had decided to flee, I wouldn't have been able to run after her with your son on my leg. It not only put me in jeopardy, but he could have been hurt." Although, it was impossible to book a five-year-old kid for obstructing. I should have booked the Mom. *Oh well*, I thought, *don't sweat the small stuff. It's all in a day's work.*

CHAPTER 12
So Called Friends

As Red picked up Friday's newspaper, he saw a familiar face on the front page. It was his pilot friend, Brad. He had been arrested for smuggling drugs out of Mexico. As Red continued reading, he was shocked. Brad had been smuggling drugs for years by private aircraft. Red recalled going to Chihuahua twice and Hermosillo once in his own plane. Brad evidently used Red three times to bring the drugs into the United States in our airplane. If caught, Red would have NEVER convinced the DEA or border patrol of his innocence.

Truly he was totally unaware of his friend's underhanded, illegal dealings. Our plane would have been confiscated, and Red would be in a Mexican jail to this very day or a U.S. Federal Prison. The whole scenario was scary to think about. Our entire lives would have been in shambles. How could Brad do such a thing? I wondered if his wife was aware of his underhanded dealings. Brad was going to federal prison for a long time. I'm so thankful that Red was not taken down with him. There really are some innocent people incarcerated.

Red had lost contact with Brad when he went to work for the police department. *Gee, I wonder why?* Red had our plane up for sale. He would still rent it occasionally, but it didn't bring in enough to make the monthly payments, insurance, maintenance or the hangar fee. Red started thinking back to the times he flew to Mexico. He remembered the little grass airstrip in the middle of nowhere. He thought about the times that Brad would be discussing business in almost a whisper. Red recalled that usually the day after their return to North Las Vegas Air Terminal, Brad would call and need the keys to the plane, because he forgot his sunglasses or briefcase. Now as a cop Red could put it all together. *Brad was unloading the drugs from the plane, but where was he hiding them?* Red thought. He was crushed that a good friend he had respected was really a bad guy who took advantage of their so-called friendship. *You just can't tell a book by its cover,* Red thought.

That was not the end of trusting good friends. Red had a close friend that was also a pilot. They had often flown together, hung out at the airport, and went to all the airshows. Red knew Rob for over thirty-five years. Rob was in real estate and had given us good tips from time to time. He wanted us to invest with him on an eight-apartment complex. The buy in was $100,000. We had half that amount saved, but it had taken us years to put that much aside. We had been so thrifty. The savings was going to be what Red referred to as our "rocking chair" money, not to be touched. That was emergency money to use if necessary, after we had retired on our fixed income. We made payments to Rob for the other $50,000 until it was paid off.

But after investing with Rob the real estate market started to decline. We kept on paying until our $100,000 investment was complete. One awful day, Rob came to us to say that he had declared bankruptcy. Without any warning, our investment was gone. I couldn't get over how nonchalantly he put it. That money was everything we had put aside, since we both had been working. How could he do that to us? He still called from time to time, but I had a hard time talking to him or being friendly. Rob eventually made all his money back in an upswing of the real estate market and is a rich man today, but we never saw a penny of our investment that he said was a safe bet. He considered our dealings just business. "Win a few, loose a few." We certainly didn't see it that way. He said he was sorry, but his apology came too late. "If you can't trust your friends, then who can you trust?"

I remember telling Red about an incident after being on the police department for three weeks. He thought it was comical, but not me. It wasn't a serious monetary loss, or a friendship ended like he had experienced. It was simply an embarrassment to me. My co-workers didn't give me the heads up, and I ended up looking like a fool. I was just getting my feet wet, so to speak. Briefing was almost finished, so I put the hot sheet on my clipboard where it was easily accessible. Already I had gotten a hit on a stolen car, boosting my confidence a bit. As I headed to the parking garage to check out my vehicle, the sergeant called, "Beal, don't leave yet. I want to talk to you." As he caught up with me, he said, "I haven't heard of you giving any road side assistance. Have you changed a tire, yet?"

"No Sarge, I didn't think that was part of my job."

"Don't be a smart ass," he barked. "Assist a motorist this shift, be a well-rounded officer." Then he threw a pair of coveralls at me. Half way through my shift, I spotted a pregnant woman along the road with a flat tire on her Volkswagen.

"Control, 2 John 4, I'm out with a WFA (White female adult) on 95 North near the Sahara exit. Nevada Plate CRE743, Blue VW bug.

"Control copied."

I slipped into the coveralls and walked up to the woman in distress. I couldn't find the jack or a spare tire. I was hoping that no robbery went down in my area, while I was on this assignment. I heard another unit call the sergeant to respond to North 95 at Sahara exit. The sergeant asked, "Is there a problem?"

"Charlie 523, you've got to see this!"

Wait a minute, I thought, *that's my location. What's the big deal? Do I have to actually prove that I was going to change a tire? Maybe this is a set up and I fell for it. We have crime to fight and people to protect, not jokes to play on rookies.* Another unit called control and was out at the same location. *Oh, no,* I thought, *is this car on the hot sheet, and I missed it? Lord, please don't let me be assisting a car thief!*

When the sergeant arrived, he walked up quickly to my side and angrily whispered, "What in the hell are you doing?"

"Trying to assist a motorist, sir. Isn't that what you wanted me to do?"

"Yes, stupid, but not in prison coveralls. I gave those to you to return to the jail per normal operating procedure, not to wear them, you fool."

"Sarge, you didn't make that clear. When you threw me the coveralls, I thought you meant for me to wear them when I changed a tire."

"Who do you think you are? Some kind of garage mechanic that needs to slip on coveralls to protect his clothes? I'm surprised that people passing by aren't calling the police station to advise of an escaped convict on the side of the freeway. Now get those damn things off and take them directly to jail. I'll have another unit change the tire."

When I looked up, there were now two more patrol units parked along the freeway, gawking at me, and laughing hysterically. I thought it was so nice that I could make their day. I headed to my patrol car, smiled at the other units, and then flipped them off. Didn't they have anything better to do? It must have been a slow night in their areas.

Not until I took off the coveralls did I see the stencil on the back HIGH DESERT STATE PRISON. Oops.

The first unit could have given me the heads up without calling the sergeant, but then that wouldn't have been any fun. I guess there's a secret creed, "let's not help rookies. Let's make them look like idiots." Well, it worked.

The public had a hard time adjusting to female officers on patrol. Many times, I would get in fights and there would be no unit to back me up. A male would back up another male unit, but not me. The sergeant said it was because he wanted to see if I could handle the call by myself. There was a double standard.

Red blamed his involvement with the union on the problems I was having with the police department. He said that management was getting even with him through attacks on me. I told him, "Do not worry about me. Just keep fighting for the good hours, wages, and working conditions for the officers." Yes, I fought City Hall, and I took them to court but to no avail. I'll skip all the drama of the case, because I don't want it to sound like sour grapes. They tried to fire me, but according to their own policy, they had to send me back to the job I had before becoming an officer. I went back to the airport, and quickly put in an application for airport operations coordinator. It was a position to inspect runways, respond to emergency landings, plane crashes, bomb threats, and to handle hijackings. I got the job and an eleven step pay increase. When one door closes another one opens.

CHAPTER 13
The Trial

On March 4th, 1980, at age 42, Red was shot in the head. Two of his fellow officers came to the house shortly after midnight to advise me of the incident. We sued Smith & Wesson Gun Manufacturer in a civil trial in Federal Court since the gun misfired.

The following events led up to the trial, four and a half years later. We were getting packed for our vacation. I have never been to Hawaii. I guess that's why I was so excited about the trip. In just two weeks, Red and I would be lying on the warm sandy beach rubbing sun screen over our fair skinned bodies, and sipping pina coladas made with fresh pineapple juice and coconut. What a glorious week it would be with no bills to sort through, no phone calls to return, no local newspapers to read, no politics to dabble in, and, best of all, no doctor appointments.

We both needed to get away from life in the fast lane. We had worked opposite shifts for years. The only good thing about our schedule was that our kids always had an adult at home, whether it is to get them off to school or cook dinner for them. One of us was always there, half asleep sometimes, but, nevertheless, there. We left lots of notes taped on the refrigerator to remind each other of a wrestling match after school on Friday, the soccer game on Saturday, or a dentist appointment on Monday morning. Now we were going to have some quiet time together to get reacquainted.

I looked at my watch and realized that the mailman must have come, so I walked to the mailbox. I saw a car parked by our driveway and figured the man needed directions, so I went over and asked if I could help. He told me the address he was looking for and said he needed to contact the Beal's. I smiled and said "You are here and I'm Jorjan Beal." He handed me two pieces of paper, grinned, and drove off.

It read: "Greetings from the State of Nevada."

Oh great, my husband and I had just been served with a subpoena. We had waited four and a half years for this lawsuit to come to trial, and, wouldn't you know, that it arrives at vacation time. I hoped it would be over in a few days, and we could still go on our trip. After all, I couldn't get a refund on the charter flight and no refund on the room deposit.

Tuesday, October 30th, 1984, 8:30 a.m.

Federal Court, Dept. 1

Jacob Lee Beal (Red's name) v/s Smith & Wesson Corporation (a civil case)

Jury selection took ever so long. There were twenty-five people called for jury duty. Only six jurors and two alternates are needed in federal court. We sat through four hours of interviews then the process of elimination began. I watched closely as the attorneys for Smith & Wesson huddled together, whispered to each other, scrutinized each person on the list, then crossed them off, and told them they were excused. This went back and forth, with the attorneys marking off the ones they thought were either unsuitable or prejudicial. Finally, the six jurors were chosen as well as the two alternates.

The day ended with only the jury chosen. Tomorrow would be Oct. 31st, I figured there would be no court, since it was Nevada Day. I was wrong. This was federal court which doesn't recognize a state holiday.

Wednesday Oct. 31, 1984, 9:00a.m.

Federal Court Dept. 1

The Honorable Judge Lamar Allen presiding

"All rise," said the bailiff.

Our attorney approached the selected jurors, and in twenty minutes explained what he intended to prove, and which witnesses would be testifying. The defense attorney followed suit. He stood about six foot five, must have worn a size sixteen shoe, dressed conservatively, but disheveled. He was probably in his mid-fifties and came across as a pompous ass.

On the other hand, our attorney, Rubin Goldstein, a small Jewish fellow, approximately forty-two years of age, dressed spiffy, and was definitely the pick of litter. He hailed from Virginia, so he had this pleasant southern drawl. Other than his name, he neither looked nor talked like a Jew. His partner, Jack, was also Jewish, but looked Italian. He was a nice-looking man, dressed impeccably, about forty years old, from North Carolina, and also with a hint of a drawl. To the jurors an attorney's attire and demeanor can make or break a case. Rubin and Jack were not only highly intelligent, they had wit and personality to boot. I figured that gave us the edge. The defense had a battery of attorneys, some from Massachusetts and Delaware, and Mr. Delaney from Las Vegas.

I don't know what held up the proceedings, but we didn't get started until 10:45 a.m. Red was the first to be called to the stand. The clerk asked him to raise his right hand.

"Do you solemnly swear to tell the truth, the whole truth, and nothing but the truth, so help you God?"

"I do," said Red as he took a seat.

"State your full name to the court and your occupation," said Rubin.

"Jacob Lee Beal, I am a police officer in the patrol division for the Metropolitan Police Department."

"How many years have you been on the department?" asked Rubin.

"Ten years," Jacob replied.

"Will you relay the events leading up to the night of March 4, 1980," continued Rubin?

"Yes, it was shortly after midnight." said Jacob. "My partner and I were patrolling the Westside of town, which was our regularly assigned area, when we observed a brown Oldsmobile failing to stop at the stop sign. As the driver spotted us, he sped up, turned out his headlights, and quickly rounded the corner. We ran a registration check on the car. It came back stolen. We saw the vehicle pull into a driveway, and we pulled in behind it. The Oldsmobile had tinted windows. We couldn't tell how many occupants were in the car so we called them to step out of the vehicle with their hands up. Two females exited from the back seat then dashed toward the house. The driver and the passenger got out, ignoring our instructions to step in front of the police car. One darted toward the front door. I went after him. The passenger ran toward the backyard, where my partner chased him. The driver was not cooperating. He tried to jerk away from me, and the fight was on. Our feet got tangled, and we both went down to the ground. I was on my back with the black suspect straddling me. He had a death grip around my neck. Every time I tried to pull the suspect's hands away from my throat to breathe, he would grab for my gun."

As I watched Red testify, my heart went out to him. He was reliving the nightmare all over again. Maybe, we should have never sued. It wasn't worth all this hassle. Yet the gun malfunctioned. That had to be brought out in the open, so the manufacturer could recall the firearm and make it safe. Too many others were hurt. This had to stop.

In cross-examination the defense attorney, Delaney, was an ogre. He twisted and turned everything around to make the jurors think that Red was a bad police officer. He portrayed Red as prejudiced against blacks and making roust arrests. That was the farthest from the truth. I resented those accusations and underhanded tactics.

Red had been badgered on the stand for two and a half hours, and he was tired. His words were now slurring, his mouth was drawing to one side, as it often did since the shooting, and he began drooling. He would occasionally dab the corner of his mouth with his handkerchief. He rarely went anywhere without several hankies in his pocket.

It hurt me to watch him testify. Here was a man who had been so very active and vocal. Now he had problems speaking and couldn't even stand without losing his balance. I fidgeted with the scarf I had around my neck, rolling the edges back and forth. I'd squeeze my thumb in a fist then push the cuticle back with my index finger.

I was so angry with the gun manufacturer for putting out a faulty weapon, that discharged if dropped or hit, without even pulling the trigger. At times the gun would jam, not allowing the shell to eject. I knew this first hand from my experience with the weapon at the firing range, when I was a police officer. In my opinion, the nine-millimeter, model 59, semiautomatic, wasn't worth the powder to blow it up.

Can you imagine being in the midst of a shoot-out then throwing your hands up in the air with your fingers crossed, yelling "Kings X-Time out! I have to un-jam my weapon."

I can clearly imagine the response. "Yeah right Honky, Your ass is mine."

Court was adjourned for the day. At this rate the case wouldn't be concluded until Christmas. I kissed Red goodbye and headed to work. Thank goodness I was on swing shift and didn't have to take time off for the trial.

Thursday, November 1, 1984, 9:00 a.m.

Red's attorney assured us, "There will be no chance of missing your vacation."

"Thanks," I said. "That is a relief to hear. I feel better already."

Red and I were going to enjoy Hawaii. We would soon be lying under a palm tree, relaxed, knowing the trial was behind us. Meanwhile we were mentally shopping and began thinking how we would spend some of the settlement money. First, we had to reimburse the health insurance company and worker's compensation for the medical bills.

It had taken much too long for this civil case to come to court. The criminal case was two years ago, and the suspect was found NOT guilty by a jury of his peers. That gave the suspect reason to believe that he really was innocent. He decided to sue Jacob, his partner, and the police department, separately, for a million dollars. Metro didn't want the expense of a court case, so they settled the law suit out of court, like they did with so many other nuisance lawsuits. To go to court was much more costly. Red was furious that the suspect got one red cent. "No one should ever be rewarded for doing something wrong," he spouted.

Here we are in court with the gun manufacturer hoping to see justice prevail.

"The court calls Jacob Lee Beal to the stand."

Jacob took the stand again and was sworn in. No matter how hard the defense tried to turn his words around, Jacob constantly corrected Mr. Delaney. Red frowned and continually said, "No, that is not what I just said." The judge would ask the stenographer to read back the statement.

The newly appointed judge was so wishy-washy, that he was afraid to make any ruling. He had previously been a district court judge but was elevated to federal judge. I'm sure it was due to his religious background and the connections in the state. The same old politics applied. He couldn't make a decision and it became his mantra to say, "Let's just move on."

Our attorney would jump up and say, "Objection, Your Honor." But Judge Allen could not say, "Overruled" or "Sustained." Oh no, those words were not in his vocabulary. Again and again, he would reiterate, "Let's just move on."

I wanted to drive a steel spike down his spine to give him some backbone. Now on the other hand, I really liked the young law clerk who kept whispering in the judge's ear to remind him of a mistake. He knew more than the judge. I would have liked a role reversal. The clerk would often leave the courtroom and come back with law books to prove a point. This kid had moxie.

Red continued his testimony. "The suspect was sitting on top of me straddled. His hands were around my neck in a choke hold. I must have passed out for a moment for lack of oxygen but came around in time to put one hand on top of my holster, since he was going for my gun. I heard females coming out of the house yelling obscenities. Then they started kicking me. I was dizzy and gasping for air. I had no more strength left. My partner let his suspect go, when he heard me gurgling. He ran to my side, but it was too late. There was a deafening sound. It felt like my head was being driven down into the concrete driveway. My whole body jolted, and I felt an explosion in my face. The pain was excruciating, and the blood was gushing profusely. I tried to call my partner. 'Dean, I've been hit!' But I wasn't sure he heard me. I was confused. Was I just shot with my own gun? For a moment there was dead silence. Then I heard my partner on the radio calling for help. 'Send back-up. My partner's been shot,' said Dean, in a strained voice."

"I was still being kicked over and over, in my head, back and side. I tried to get up and take cover, before I got shot again, but I was too light headed. As I tried to focus, I saw an old black woman in a Mumu standing over me. She was kicking and cursing. I managed to get up on one knee, but just kept spinning around in a circle getting nowhere. I thought I was crawling for cover, but I wasn't. I heard cars squealing around the corner, then screeching to a halt. In the distance, I heard someone yell, 'Put him in the back seat of my patrol car. We don't have time to wait for the ambulance.' I was now enroute to the hospital."

"I was getting sick to my stomach and asked one of the cops to loosen my gun belt. I was quivering and ever so cold. My mind was racing, *will I make it to the hospital? Will I see my family again? Will my partner catch the suspect?"*

I was relieved when the court recessed for lunch (Not that I had any appetite). When court resumed, Red's partner, Dean, was called to testify. Dean slowly approached the stand.

"Do you solemnly swear to tell the truth, the whole truth and nothing but the truth so help you God?"

"I do," said Dean, stoically, then he sat down.

"State your full name and occupation," said Rubin.

"Dean Andrew Baker, I am a police officer for the Metropolitan Police Department."

"Where were you on the night of March 4, 1984?

"I was working graveyard shift on the Westside of Las Vegas with my partner, Jacob Beal."

"Will you relay the chain of events on that night in question?" continued Rubin.

"We observed a brown Oldsmobile run a stop sign. I ran the license plate, and it came back hot. The driver tried to evade us by turning out the headlights and speeding away. We stayed right behind him. He pulled up into a driveway and began honking the horn. Two females exited the car and ran into the house. The two males split in different directions. I chased the male passenger, and my partner went after the driver."

As Dean relayed the chain of events on that terrible night his voice began cracking. He would pause for a moment then continue.

"I looked over to see my partner on the ground. His leg was twitching, and he wasn't conscious. I saw the two females that had exited the vehicle earlier. Now they were back outside of the house and kicking Jacob. I saw an old lady spitting in his face. I let go of my suspect and ran to my partner. I pushed one of the females aside and pulled the other one away from Jacob, because she was on her knee trying to get his gun. I desperately tried to pull the suspect off of Jacob, but he was too strong, and high on what I later found to be PCP (Angel dust, an elephant tranquilizer). It was as if I was nothing but a fly. He swung me backwards, as he pivoted on one foot. A female yanked at my coat, trying to pull me down to keep me from freeing Jacob from the choke hold. I kept trying, but I was losing the battle and so was Jacob. He was gurgling more, as if his windpipe was closed off."

Then Dean stopped, took a deep breath and said, "I pulled out my gun and hit the suspect on the head, hoping to knock him out. But the gun accidentally discharged at close range, hitting my partner in the face."

Tears were streaming down Dean's face as he told what transpired on that horrible night. "I had lost my portable radio in the fight, so I ran back to the patrol car to call for paramedics and back up. I returned to Jacob, who was trying to run for cover. But he was only pivoting on one knee. I held him upright in my arms to keep him from choking further on his blood and to console him. I thought, *Thank God, for now, he is still alive.*

Dean paused again, put his hand to his mouth obviously shaken, looked out at Jacob and said, "This was not only my partner, but my best friend."

I was glad that Red couldn't see me crying. There were others in the court room emotionally distraught and blowing their noses, as well as two jurors wiping away their tears.

"What happened then?" asked Rubin.

"The suspects all fled when they heard the sirens of the backup units arriving. Two officers put Jacob in their patrol car and headed to the hospital, calling in ahead of time to advise they were enroute with an officer with a gunshot wound to the head. I stayed to search the area along with two backup units. We found the driver hiding in his mama's house and took him into custody."

It was now the defense attorney's turn to refute. He tried to crucify Dean. "Now wasn't that a touching display of emotion!" Delaney said, sarcastically. "Who do you think you are fooling?" Delaney was the one grandstanding with all the drama he could muster.

"Isn't it a fact that you pulled your weapon to shoot the suspect, and when he moved, you hit your partner instead," Delaney shouted.

"No, that is not how it was," said Dean, shaking his head.

"No further questions," said Delaney.

The court called the next witness, the gun expert who had flown in from California on Red's behalf. He had an extensive background with various weapons. He looked directly into the jury box and spoke to each juror. His testimony proved, without a shadow of a doubt, that Dean's nine-millimeter, model 59, was defective, discharging nine out of ten times, when hit against an object at a forty-five-degree angle.

Cross-examination didn't confuse the expert witness in the least. He could not be discredited. As a matter of fact, I thought his testimony would cinch the case.

Delaney referred to the gun expert as Clint Eastwood, staging a scene for sensationalism. "Yes," Delaney said, "it only happens that way in the movies, not in reality."

Delaney wanted to make a big issue of the cops not carrying their firearms on safety at all times. "These accidents wouldn't occur, if the police officers followed the rules set forth in the department policy manual."

The next witness called was the supervisor of Metro's Supply Bureau. He showed Dean's gun records, when the weapon was issued, to whom it was issued, and the serial number. He also stated that it had not been repaired or modified. He showed the chain of command since the gun was booked into evidence. All of this was just the usual formalities.

"The court calls Lt. Harris to the stand."

After being sworn in, Harris stated, "I am a training officer in the Las Vegas Metro Police Academy. "There is no department regulation requiring an officer to carry his weapon on safety. Ninety percent of the officers prefer to have the safety off, because they don't want to take their eyes off a suspect or lose concentration in a moment of excitement. It's risky business to look down at your gun to flip the safety, especially for Officer Baker who is left-handed. The safety can't be accessed with the prominent hand he uses to pull the trigger. In a life-or-death situation, every moment counts.

Delaney asked, "Lieutenant Harris, isn't it against department policy to use the weapon as a club?"

Then Harris replied, "The officer should not use the gun as a nightstick, except as a last resort to stabilize a situation, without shooting the suspect. A gun, to a policeman, is a tool. A hunter or competition pistol contestant only uses the gun to shoot. They take excellent care of their weapons. On the other hand, the cop's gun gets lots of abuse—

numerous nicks and gouges from going over fences and wrestling with suspects on the hard concrete. They must keep their weapon clean and qualify regularly at the firing range, but it's still just a tool of the trade.

"No further questions," puffed Delaney.

Court was adjourned until the next day at 9:00 a.m.

"All rise," said the bailiff, as Judge Allen left the court room.

What a long day it had been, and was not yet over, because now I was headed to work for my swing shift. My thoughts kept returning to the settlement we would receive. I knew it would not drastically change my life, just make it a little easier. I knew exactly what Red would do with the settlement. He would upgrade our motorhome to a diesel bus. I teased him about it. "You are not a country western singer yet, heading to Nashville to make recordings. You have to learn to sing and play the guitar first. You are getting the cart before the horse. You can't get a fancy tour bus, until you become a performer.

But my thoughts kept shifting back to the trial.

I worried about the defense badgering me when it was my turn to testify.

Would they be looking for skeletons in my closet?

I recalled on the first day of Red's testimony, when Delaney asked him how many children he had. Red answered, "Two sons."

Then Delaney looked at the jurors and yelled, "Officer Beal just stated that he has two sons when in fact he only has one. Isn't that true? The other one is adopted."

"Yes," stated Jacob. "Nevertheless, I still have two sons."

Delaney said, "Don't play games with me. When I ask you how many children you have, don't skirt the issue. Tell me the truth." Now we are arguing semantics and he made Red look like a liar. Of course, that was Delaney's game plan. The jury, implicitly, understood Red's reply.

The judge hit the gavel, bringing my mind back to the present. "Court adjourned, until Monday, November 5, 8:30 a.m. "Would the attorney's meet me in my chambers?" asked Judge Allen.

What did this mean? What happened to Thursday and Friday of this week? What was going on? We sat in the courtroom until our attorney's returned. Rubin explained that the judge would be out of town for several days and the trial would resume on Monday. Oh, No. They were cutting this too close to our vacation. Our attorney assured us that we should be finished Tuesday at the latest.

"But our trip is next Friday, the ninth," I frowned.

"Not to worry," said Rubin Goldstein.

How nice it would be to get away, and celebrate the end of this trial, and all the bad memories. It was up to the jurors to set the amount for the settlement. I felt confident that the jurors would decide on the figure asked, since it wasn't exorbitant. We knew that by winning the case we would have to reimburse the worker's compensation for paying all the medical bills which totaled $100,000. That is why we were asking for a half million dollars in a settlement. That was not what we considered outrageous—not for all the pain and suffering Red went through. He would have problems the rest of his life. On the other hand, if we lost, which we had never dwelt upon, we would not have to pay back workers compensation. But just the witness fees alone would be high. The gun expert charged $40,000 to testify, plus travel expenses. There would be the charges by the doctors, as if they were doing surgery for the day. The dentists charged an hourly rate, plus travel time. The attorney fees went back four and a half years for depositions, letters written, phone calls made plus other communications. Last, but not least, there were the court costs. I shuttered when I thought of the cost of the total bill. It would look more like the national debt. Since this was a civil case, we didn't go to the union to pay for representation. Two years ago, the police union handled the criminal case which only lasted two days when the suspect, Rummel, was found not guilty by a jury of his peers for attempted murder. Trying to choke Red to death didn't count. What a shame. That was a travesty of justice.

Court seemed to drag on and on—Monday, Tuesday, Wednesday. There were too many recesses, the lunch breaks were too long, and often the judge would ask to meet with counsel in his chambers. I was glad I was packed for Hawaii, because we planned to leave in two days.

Thursday, Nov.8, 1984, 9:00 a.m.

Dr. Keys, the neurologist, was supposed to testify first this morning, but he wasn't there. I wondered if he had a last-minute emergency. Rubin turned to me and said, "Jorjan, you will have to testify next since Dr. Keys isn't here."

My heart sunk to my feet. I was supposed to testify last so I could tie all the loose ends together. Oh, this wasn't good. I would have to appear calm and collected, not lose my composure. I needed to focus, and not let Delaney get the best of me. My heart was pounding so hard, I was glad that I was wearing a suit jacket instead of a sweater. No one would be able to see my chest heaving from my nervousness.

"The court calls Jorjan Beal to the stand." I was sworn in and sat down with hands tightly folded to keep them from shaking.

"Mrs. Beal, would you relay the events of March 4, 1980," said Rubin.

"Yes. My husband worked graveyard shift, so when I was awakened after midnight by a knock-on the door, I didn't think anything of it. I thought he had forgotten his subpoena for court the following day. I hurried downstairs to let him in by removing the safety chain. As I peeked out the window, I saw two officers. Still, I thought they probably came by to get Jacob's paperwork for court the following morning, since he was probably on a lengthy call.

I knew both officers, and they weren't acting right. I remembered one starred down at his boots. The other tried to speak but was hemming and hawing around. He finally said, "There's been an accident, and Jacob has

been shot. We are here to take you to the hospital." "How bad is it?" I asked, nervously.

They either didn't know yet or didn't want to tell me.

"Where was he hit?" I softly asked.

"In the head," said one of the officers.

Oh, now I was visualizing Red with diminished mental capacity. Then I asked who shot him, but they ignored the question and went on to advise that the suspect was in custody. Being a police officer, that is what we always want to hear, "Suspect in custody." I quickly dressed and left a short note for the boys, in case they woke in the middle of the night looking for me. I didn't mention that their Dad was shot. I would do that when I assessed his condition and came back for them. They were of high school age. They were well aware that, with both parents being police officers, anything can happen at any time or any place. I'm sure that was not a very comforting position to be in.

When I arrived at the hospital, I became edgy seeing so much brass standing in the hallway. There stood the Sheriff, the undersheriff, the watch commander, the deputy chiefs, captains, lieutenants, sergeants and many of the rank and file. I wondered, *it is the middle of the night. What are they all doing here?* They looked so somber and all nodded to me as I was rushed into the emergency room where Dr. Singleton was working on Red. We both knew the doctor because she was dating a police officer. I knew most of the staff at the hospital emergency room, because I volunteered once a week for the rape crisis center, counseling rape victims. Dr. Singleton was so sweet to come over and stand behind me so I wouldn't pass out. Unbelievably, Red had the where-with-all to warn her ahead of time that I get sick at the sight of blood—not a good trait for a cop but something I

overcame through hypnosis. Dr. Singleton had thoughtfully covered up the left side of his face with a towel because it had been blown away.

"It's important," she said, "that he sees you and knows that you are here." I moved closer to the gurney and picked up his hand and squeezed it. The doctor moved a chair to the side of the bed.

"Hi Hon," I said in an attempt to sound cheery. Red tried to talk but he had all sorts of twitches pulling his mouth to the side and he was barely audible.

Dr. Singleton said, "The neurosurgeon has just arrived, and he needs to put Jacobs's facial nerves and muscles back together."

Jacob kept asking how extensive the injuries were and was there brain damage. He also wanted to know how much of his face was gone. He squeezed my hand tighter and said, "Sweet, I don't want to be a vegetable."

I was so thankful that he recognized me. His cognitive thinking didn't seem to be damaged.

Dr. Singleton said, "He can't close his left eye, and the x-rays showed his jaw is broken in eight places. Believe it or not, he bit down as the bullet went into his jaw, and it slowed the velocity. Yes, he literally 'bit the bullet,' but it ripped out half of his teeth. Part of the bullet lodged in the back of the head, one quarter of an inch above his spinal column. The casing of the bullet went through the back of his ear." Then Dr. Singleton said, "I need you to scoot out of here for now, so the neurosurgeon can work on him."

One of the officer's drove me home, because I wanted to wake the boys and return to the hospital with them as soon as possible. I think Red felt he might die. I wanted to be there to reassure him that all the doctors were working hard and doing what was necessary to stabilize him. Of course, the most important part of any crisis is prayer. There was a lot of that! But back to the courtroom—Our attorney, Rubin, looked to the back of the courtroom and said, "Your Honor, Dr. Keys has just arrived. I would like to call him to the stand, so he can get back to his patients at the hospital. I would like to recall Mrs. Beal later."

"Okay, let's just move on," said the judge in his usual mantra. Dr. Keys was sworn in. State your full name and occupation.

"I am Dr. Michael Matthew Keys, a neurosurgeon." "How did you come to know Jacob Beal?" Said Rubin.

I was called to Southern Nevada Memorial Hospital on March 5th, 1984, shortly after midnight. Officer Beal had been shot in the face at close range.

Can you tell us the extent of his injuries? Continued Rubin.

"Yes, Jacob's jaw had been shattered in eight places. His teeth were sheared off, and his facial nerves and muscles were all bunched together in the back of his head. His left eye bulged and would not close. The bullet had lodged in the back of his neck, just a quarter of an inch from his spinal column. I worried that it might paralyze him, if it shifted. The casing of the bullet was in his left ear near the mastoid bone causing the loss of hearing. There were fragments of bullet throughout his head. His left saliva gland was destroyed. He needed radiation treatments to keep it from eating out the inside of his mouth. He had two additional surgeries, one to remove the casing from his ear, and the second to later remove the bullet from the back of his head. There were twenty-six follow-up visits to me during his convalescing, and one year of facial therapy that followed to get his jaw opened. It was touch and go at first, because I didn't know if any of the blood vessels were going to erupt and explode in his head. What a tough man, Officer Beal is. He never complained. He was a good and cooperative patient in every way. But he didn't like hospitals and negotiated with me each time to let him go home early, saying that he could recover faster at the house. He was right."

Dr. Keyes left his compassionate delivery behind for the jurors to maul over. I watched the jurors closely and knew that they liked him. Two other doctors had arrived to give their testimony.

"The court calls Dr. Nickolas Gimelli to the stand," said the bailiff. "State your full name and your occupation."

"My name is Dr. Nickolas Anthony Gimelli, and I am an orthopedic surgeon. I performed two back surgeries on Officer Beal's lower lumbar region due to shattered discs from being kicked over and over."

"Objection," yelled Delaney. "The doctor wasn't there to see what happened."

"Let's just move on," said Judge Allen. The testimony went on for quite a while. I hoped that the doctors could finish and get back to their patients before the court adjourned.

"The court calls Dr. William Schiff to the stand. "Do you swear to tell the truth the whole truth and nothing but the truth so help you God."

"I do."

"Please state your full name and occupation."

"My name is Dr. William Carl Schiff, I am a dentist." "How did you come to know Officer Beal?" asked Rubin.

"He had been in a shooting incident, and half his teeth were sheared off by the bullet. He came to my office a year later on March 5, 1981. The work on his teeth was extensive. He had bitten down as the bullet ripped through his mouth, this slowed the velocity enough to lessen the damage. He was my patient for two years. My initial problem was trying to get his mouth open. It was frozen shut with only a small opening, so I could not open his mouth to exam the damage. My first attempt at an examination cracked his jawbone in half, breaking it at one of the weak points that hadn't healed correctly. But something had to be done, because his teeth were abscessing, and the poison was going throughout his body. It could have killed him." "Recess for lunch." *Halleluiah*

After the lunch break, Rubin stated, "I would now like to recall Mrs. Beal to the stand." I was sworn in again.

Rubin asked, "How did Jacob look and feel while he was in the hospital?"

"He looked terrible! There were tubes hanging out of jaw, his ear, his nose, and his mouth. He was being fed intravenously. The tube in his jaw was draining the saliva gland, so the acid wouldn't eat out his mouth from the inside. He had radiation treatment on the left side of his jaw which caused some of his hair and sideburn to fall out."

I thought to myself, *When it grew back in, later, it was gray. Had he entered the annual Helldorado Rodeo beard contest, he would have won for having the most unique beard. It was like drawing a line down the middle of his head and face. One side of his hair, sideburn and whiskers were red, the other side was gray. He was the two-toned man.*

"He was hooked up to a heart monitor because of an irregular beat due to the trauma. He couldn't walk without assistance, not only was he weak but he had damage to his ear. He had lost his equilibrium."

The boys and I stayed with him except to go home to shower and change clothes. The nurses had to keep the troves of visitors away, so he could get some rest. Red had worked the black area of town on grave shift for ten years. He knew most of the people there and their families. Red had been raised in a poor desolate part of Oklahoma. He could relate to most of these folks—the hard-working ones—not the thugs and dope dealers.

"When he was able to come home, I was scared to death. I thought it was too soon. He still had a tube sticking out of the face. He continued to bleed from the ear, face and mouth. After changing his bandages, I would go into the bathroom and vomit. I kept saying to myself, I can do this, I can, I can. With God's help, anything is possible."

Feeding him was difficult. He couldn't eat solid food for a year. He lived on juices and high protein drinks. He would force a straw into the side of his mouth, where he had teeth missing, then hold the other side of his mouth, so the liquid wouldn't run back out. He had a lot of trouble swallowing because of being choked so badly. Eventually he graduated to watered down baby food. His squad bought him a food processor, but when meat is pulverized, it has the same taste and consistency as liver, and he sure didn't like that.

His breath smelled so badly," but he couldn't help it. He could barely get a Q-Tip in his mouth with lemon juice on it to clean his teeth."

Rubin asked, "Could you relate the differences before the shooting compared to afterward."

"Prior to the incident, we would go out dancing, swimming, riding dune buggies through the desert, and flying our own plane to visit family. Now he can't walk straight without running into the walls. It hurts him to see me carry in the groceries, take out the garbage, carry in firewood, or get the ladder out to trim trees. He can barely walk, let alone climb a ladder. He sleeps downstairs, because he can't walk upstairs to the master bedroom. He can't even lean over to get the newspaper in the morning without falling over. He can't lean over to get a drink from a water fountain without getting dizzy and nauseated.

He can't fly his plane anymore, because he can't pass the physical. So he put it up for sale. When he gave up his private and commercial pilot's license, it broke his heart. Jacob had worked so hard to get all the ratings. He wanted to teach his sons to fly. But that was a promise he will never be able to keep.

He couldn't even pass his police physical, so he will never be allowed to go back to the streets in the patrol division. Instead, he was assigned to work behind a desk to shuffle papers and take complaint calls, which nearly drives him nuts. He has always been an active man, so being stuck behind a desk is sheer torture.

We don't go to restaurants to eat because of the limitations in opening his mouth. His diet is restricted. He can't eat anything sticky like peanut butter, because he no longer has a saliva gland to help process and dissolve the food. And forget about ordering a BLT, submarine, whooper, or eating corn on the cob. He can't open his mouth that wide. It was four years before he could eat a steak. He can't yawn or whistle, anymore.

Romantically speaking, we have had our share of problems. Anytime he leans over, he gets sick to his stomach. Throwing up in bed can quickly quell the fire of passion. That is physically and psychologically damaging to both of us. There are other ramifications too personal for a courtroom, but, to sum it up, lovemaking which was once a high priority is now at the bottom of the list. He has nightmares and yells out in the night which is unnerving. He's jumpy around loud bangs, and once knocked me right off the curb when a car backfired. Due to his hearing loss, the radio and TV are so loud that I have to leave the room for sanity's sake.

You asked how it has changed our lives. It's been stifling, and a complete role reversal. At work I traded swing shift for graveyard shift, so I could be home to take him to the many doctor appointments over the span of the last four and a half years. Before his first back surgery, the boys would come home from school at noon, and help me get him up on his feet, so he could go to the bathroom. I had to feed him on the floor with a tray of food like I was feeding a dog. That was a shame, but he couldn't sit up. I took a risky promotion at work so I could earn more money in the event that I had to be the sole bread winner."

I thought to myself, *How much the boys have helped by doing the painting, repairs and lawn work. They do so much around the house and the rental apartments. They even change a flat tire for me, but I have to remember they have their own lives to live and they will not always be around. I have to learn to fend for myself and for Red.*

On cross examination, Delaney was sarcastic and snide. "Why did officer Beal go back to work just three months after the incident? He couldn't be very sick if he went back to work that soon."

"It was a diversion for him to be around others," I said. "It helped take his mind off the pain, as well as keep his mind active. He does not take pain pills, because he has a fear of becoming addicted. Yes, he went back to work even with a bullet still in the back of his head. He didn't want to go out on a disability and give up his career. Furthermore, until March 4th, 1980, he never took a sick day off work. That was a record for anyone who had been in the department for ten years."

"How do you know what pain he is in?" retorted Delaney.

"Because we have been married over twenty years, and I know him well. I walked into the kitchen and find him holding his ear. He, unaware of my presence, is grimacing with pain. I catch him holding his face, when he doesn't think I am around. His face would twitch badly from the nerve damage. He never complains, but I see these things."

"Oh, come on now, are you trying to tell me that he wasn't on pain medication?"

"No Sir," I answered. "While he was in the hospital he took pain medication, but not after coming home. I am telling you, Mr. Delaney, he was not on any pain pills at home. There were prescriptions written but never filled. You can check with the pharmacy. You see, Mr. Delaney, my husband had never taken an aspirin in his life. The only time he went to a doctor was for a broken arm as a kid, his army physical, pilot's physical, and police physical. That was until the shooting. Since that time, he's been to at least seventeen different doctors and physical therapists, sometimes two or three different appointments a day. He has had five surgeries. He had one entire year of therapy, five days a week to get his mouth opened, and physical therapy for months on his back. He had two years of dental reconstruction. He has had more than his share of suffering and pain."

The jurors glared at Delaney for being such a tyrant. Court just dragged on and on. It was inevitable that we were going to miss our trip to Hawaii. I had been packed for two weeks. I thought, *Oh well, when the court case is over, I'll reschedule our trip.*

Delaney called his next witness. "Will Lawrence Rummel take the stand?"

I thought, *Oh wait a minute," This can't be. He's in prison on drug charges and couldn't get out for a civil case.* Then a tall, nice looking, well dressed, black man walked in the court room, took the stand, and was sworn in.

"State your name," said Delaney. "Lawrence Rummel," he said, articulating well.

I looked over at our attorney shaking my head to indicate, *no, that's not him! Rummel is a low-life, nappy haired doper,* I whispered to Rubin.

The judge hit the gavel and demanded silence. Delaney continued until I jumped up and said, "Who is this imposter?"

The judge slammed the gavel several times hard and warned, "One more outbreak from you, Mrs. Beal, and I'll hold you in contempt of court!"

The witness continued until Rubin asked to approach the bench, with Delaney close on his heels. "What's going on? Is this Lawrence Rummel or not?" said Rubin.

"Wait a minute," said the judge, "This isn't Rummel? I'm confused."

Delaney turned to Rubin and said, "This gentleman is reading his deposition. Don't you remember? I said that I was going to have Lawrence

Rummel's deposition read. Did you misunderstand?" asked Delaney, sarcastically.

Rubin angrily said, "Why did he swear in by the name of Lawrence Rummel when in fact he's not? What kind of a scam are you trying to pull?"

The court clerk and the stenographer both said, "Judge Allen, can you start again? We are confused, too."

The judge excused the jury until this could be sorted out. He said he didn't want the jury to be prejudiced by this. An hour later the jury was recalled. The judge folded his hands as if in a prayer meeting and said, "Mr. Rummel couldn't be with us today so instead we will have his deposition read."

I wanted to yell, *He can't be here because Rummel is in prison!* But I didn't want to be ejected from the courtroom, or worse yet, thrown in jail for contempt of court, as threatened previously. Oh, how I wished that the judge was competent. He allowed testimony that should never have been allowed, and we couldn't say anything, not to mention all the hours wasted because he couldn't make a decision.

Rummel's deposition was read, by the nice-looking black man that originally posed as Rummel. But it was full of lies. Rummel wasn't present so there could be no cross examination.

Delaney called his next witness to the stand. "Ms. Clara Porter."

A heavy-set black woman approached wearing a bandana around her head and a beige knit dress, three sizes too small, and full of stains.

"Do you swear to tell the truth, the whole truth and nothing but the truth so help you God?"

"I do."

"What is your relationship to this case?" Delaney asked.

"Lawrence Rummel be my son." Then she looked upward with outstretched arms and began yelling, "Oh Lord, Oh Lord, them po-lice done tried to kill my son. My son ain't done nuthin' to nobody an' you knows that, Lord." She then looked at the jurors and said, "They done shot my son, an' he had to go to the hospital."

Ms. Porter was confused about who was shot, and she perjured herself eight times. Our attorney later reminded the jury that her son went to the hospital for a laceration on the head when Officer Baker hit him with the butt of the gun. He was not shot. Then our attorney said, "I'm surprised he felt anything as high as he was." "Objection," shouted Delaney.

The judge looked over at the stenographer and said, "Strike that last sentence."

"Did you kick officer Beal?" asked Rubin.

She turned away from the attorney to face the judge. "Oh no, judge, I be a

Christian all my life."

Rubin asked her, Where is your son today. She refused to answer.

Of course, Delaney jumped up and yelled, "Objection!"

Our attorney could not tell the court that, out of her son's thirty-five years on earth, he had been in and out of prison most of his life. He only did five years for killing a gasoline attendant who had five children. He shot him over a dispute for a two-cent deposit on a pop bottle. He was not supposed to leave the gas station with the bottle. When the attendant told him to leave it, Rummel got mad, went home, got a gun and came back and killed him. That was a premeditated murder. Rummel's story was different. He said that he put his money in the pop machine and the wrong brand came out. Either way, you don't kill someone over that! He also had fifteen felony arrests, and would be back on the street next year, after doing time for drug charges. Rubin was not allowed to mention that Rummel was not only suing us but Jacob's partner, Dean, as well. After all, Dean had violated his civil rights by taking him to jail. He also had a suit against the police department for a million dollars. Rummel had done less time in jail than Jacob did in surgery. The reason he was jailed was for attempted murder—trying to strangle Jacob to death.

Next Delaney brought up Rummel's criminal case two years ago where a jury of his peers found him NOT guilty on the attempted murder charge of Jacob.

In later years, Jacob referred to Rummel as another OJ Simpson, getting off free of charges on the criminal case by a jury of his peers.

Delaney called his next witness, a gun expert from Springfield, Massachusetts. I thought he was boring and ineffective.

Following that testimony, Delaney called another gun expert. He was the designer of the Smith & Wesson, model #59. The jurors listened to him more attentively. He didn't deny or admit that the gun would discharge if dropped. But he said, "It is necessary to always keep the gun on safety."

I thought to myself, *This gun manufacturer sells to hundreds of police departments throughout the United States. The gun designer wouldn't say anything derogatory to make himself look bad, or to lose all the business.*

Rubin stood in front of the designer of the gun and said, "Isn't it your responsibility and obligation to warn police officers of the dangers of your weapon discharging? Why are you shirking your duty?" Rubin then asked if it would be difficult to put a safety switch on the opposite side of the gun for all the left-handed officers.

The designer admitted, "It would be a simple process that any amateur gunsmith could do for several dollars in cost."

"Then why," Rubin asked, "hasn't your company done this for officers like Dean Baker, who are left-handed and carry the gun off safety?"

"Tradition," said the gun designer, "Since 1908, the company has made safeties on one side only—for the right-handed people. The left-handed officer must learn to be ambidextrous."

"The model #59 came out in 1978," said Rubin. How many weapons had to be recalled?"

"Objection!" shouted Delaney. He didn't want the jury to hear that number.

The judge couldn't say "Overruled." He simply said, "Let's just move on."

Thoughts swirled through my mind. *What about the innocent people shot and killed by accidental discharges when the gun was dropped. I remembered one of Metro's traffic officers pushing a stalled car out of the intersection, when his gun came out of the holster and hit the pavement. His safety was off. A little girl walking along the sidewalk was hit in the leg. I certainly thought that these cases should be brought out into the open, but, oh no, not according to Judge Allen. They would be prejudicial. The judge keeps allowing Delaney to discredit Red and Dean as bad police officers who rousted blacks and made humbug arrests. And that's not prejudicial? "Oh please, give me a break! How blatant can it be?"*

Delaney angrily shouted, "The only reason Jacob Beal was shot that night was the fact that his partner had his finger on the trigger to shoot Rummel, but Lawrence Rummel moved, and Officer Beal was shot instead. Delaney looked directly at the only black woman in the jury box hoping to gain her approval.

Delaney was wrong. It backfired because she would turn her head. When Rummel's mother testified she only looked at the black juror hoping she would side with her. Wrong again, the juror shook her head in disgust at the many times Clara Porter perjured herself.

The next day we heard the summation by each attorney. Delaney began by giving a pathetic example to prove to the jury that the gun manufacturer was not liable. He stated, "If I dug a big hole in my backyard, and I warned my neighbor to be careful because the hole was there, and he fell in the hole anyway, I wouldn't be liable. I told him about the hole."

Rubin retorted, "Well Delaney, at least you warned the neighbor of the situation. That's more than Smith & Wesson did. Therefore, they are liable of negligence. They have a defective product yet haven't warned the public about it. They haven't recalled it or made any changes to the gun. How many others are going to get hurt before this is corrected?"

Next, Judge Allen gave instructions to the jurors. I was shocked by how many instructions he cited! He gave 52 instructions. It took over one and a half hours. He warned the jurors to only go on the evidence presented. He cautioned them to not go on any gut feelings or sympathy. Judge Allen would say one thing then retract it. He would inform them of another instruction, then delete that, and state another dubious rule to be followed. Not only were the jurors confused, but so was everyone else in the courtroom. It was overwhelming. Our attorneys kept shaking their heads in disbelief.

Judge Allen informed the jurors that once they answered the questions presented by the instructions they would then each fill out a piece of paper answering the following questions: (He warned again that they had to follow the instructions implicitly.)

1. Does the jury find Smith and Wesson guilty? (Yes or no)
2. If ruled in favor of the plaintiff, how much compensation should be awarded?

3. Does the jury find the Metropolitan Police Department or any of
    its employees at fault? If so, by what percentage?

Rubin jumped up "Objection, your Honor!"

Judge Allen said, "Objection to what?"

Rubin retorted, "The last question, your Honor."

"Let's just move on," said Judge Allen, adding, "Smith & Wesson attorneys requested that this question be on the form, and I see no problem with it."

Rubin and his partner, Jack, were furious.

The jury was sequestered at 2:30 p.m. We waited in the hallway for the verdict. I felt so calm. It was over. The past three weeks had been grueling, but now I felt comfortable, even confident, that we would win. Smith & Wesson would be found negligent.

During the trial I had closely watched the jurors—how they reacted to long recesses, certain testimony, how they disliked Delaney's badgering. I observed what they wore. I knew they were conservative. I knew they would award a fair settlement.

Rubin and Jack paced back and forth in the hallway. "You just never know about a jury," said Rubin.

But deep inside I knew, and I wasn't worried. The trial was long, but we were definitely the winners.

A 5:00 p.m. the court clerk stepped into the hallway and announced, "You can all go home. Court will resume at 8:30 tomorrow."

Oh great, I thought, *now we are playing the waiting game."* I headed to work, wishing that I knew the amount of settlement we would get. But I needed to be patient. I will find out tomorrow. It was midnight when I got home from work, but Red wasn't there. I fixed a snack and a cup of coffee and waited for him. Finally, at 4:00 a.m., he came home very drunk. It had been a hectic three weeks, and he had been reliving the whole nightmare. His partner, Dean had become a full-fledged alcoholic since the shooting. We were still close friends, of course. Actually, I was glad that it was Dean who shot my husband, and not Lawrence Rummel. In that case our sons might have gone to the Westside looking for Rummel to even the score. And that never has a good outcome.

Finally, it was Decision Day. We were in court at 8:30, but the jury didn't come into the courtroom until ten o'clock. There were four females and two males. All were over the age of fifty-five except one female. She had been voted foreman. She handed the law clerk a large gold envelope. He, in turn, handed it to Judge Allen, who opened it and read it silently without any expression. The judge then handed it to the court clerk to read.

"We the jury find the defendant, Smith & Wesson, NOT GUILTY."

My heart sunk to my feet. I couldn't believe what I just heard, but I never blinked an eye, nor did I gasp, cry, or show any emotion.

The judge stood up as the bailiff said, "All rise." Judge Allen walked out.

"Court is adjourned."

I looked at Red and reached out to hold his hand. Rubin had tears in his eyes. He shook Red's hand and apologized, saying, "You just never know about a jury. You can appeal if you would like. You have thirty days in which to file."

I thought, *How on earth could we afford to appeal? This not only hurt us emotionally and physically, but now, financially. We will have to sell one of our rental properties to pay the court costs.*

Rubin said, "Even if you win the appeal they could then appeal to a higher court, and you may never see the end of it in your lifetime. They are a big corporation with lots of money and attorneys and can hold out longer than you."

Red and I looked at each other and said, "We want no more of this."

In retrospect I think that the jurors were overwhelmed with fifty-two instructions to follow. Never have I heard of so many rules they had to follow. I think that it not only confused the jurors but intimidated them. This was the first time for any of them to have been picked for a jury per their pretrial interviews, so the whole process of how the system worked may have been too much for them. It even confused our attorneys, and they have been in court hundreds of times.

For a while, I had the opportunity to dream of a nice settlement, an imaginary shopping spree, and a long-awaited vacation, but it wasn't meant to be. A settlement wouldn't put Red back together again. I have always been an optimist, but I realized this time I had been over confident in the outcome of the trial.

For Smith & Wesson the trial was over, for the attorneys it was over, but for Red it was far from over. He would suffer daily with pain and disabilities for the rest of his life from that horrible night, when a driver decided he didn't have to abide by the rules. That man could do as he damn well pleased which included running a stop sign, refusing to step in front of the police car, and choking an officer. (By the way, the car that came back on the hot sheet as stolen was really Rummel's. He had filed a stolen car report when his girlfriend absconded with it. A few days later he got the car back but failed to cancel the stolen vehicle report.)

I asked myself, *What are we to learn from this court room experience? I think I know the answer. Life is more than winning a lawsuit. Red's life is worth millions and I will thank God every day for that.*

Red could not go back to the streets as a patrol officer, so he ran for president of the police union and won. The rest of his career was spent in that position and lobbying for public safety in the legislature.

His partner joined AA and became sober. He left the police department and moved to a small town in northern Nevada.

Lawrence Rummel spent most of his time in and out of prison. He was a habitual criminal and drug addict, disrupting families and upsetting many decent people's lives. But the sun shines on the just AND the unjust—so goes the old Pennsylvania Dutch proverb. And it always will. I was shocked to learn later that when he got out of jail for the umpteenth time, he married a friend and fellow co-worker of mine from the airport. Either he turned his life around, or she turned a blind eye to him.

CHAPTER 14
Front Desk

While Red recuperated from his injuries, he worked the front desk at the police station. He knew that he could never go back to patrol. Being shot in the head took its toll on him. He couldn't imagine working at the desk the rest of his career. He didn't like all the paperwork of taking reports and registering guns.

Most people came to the police department's front desk to complain about petty things such as their neighbor's dog barking, someone parking in front of their driveway, or their teenager not staying home when grounded. Today was no different except for a mentally challenged, homeless man who refused to leave until he spoke to Mr. Secret Witness. Officer Beal asked him to step aside, so others could approach the counter, but he wouldn't budge. The man leaned over to whisper something in Red's ear. He smelled so badly Red had to back up.

All that Red could understand was "espionage papers and proof of a conspiracy." Supposedly, this information was in a small paper bag he held in his hand. The man said that the only person that could see this evidence was Mr. Secret Witness. Red tried to explain to the man that Secret Witness was a program not a person. He was getting nowhere with this explanation and the line of restless people wanting to file complaints was getting longer. "Wait over to the side of the counter and I'll see what I can do for you," said Red, as he turned to walk into the shift commander's office and explain the situation.

The commander said, "Give me three minutes then bring the man to my office." The desk sergeant took over while Red escorted the mentally challenged man to the commander's office. When they walked in, guess who was sitting behind the desk? Yes, it was Mr. Secret Witness.

Good Lord, thought Red, when he saw the commander in disguise. He had a brown paper bag over his head with two round holes cut for the eyes. Red nearly lost his composure. He bit his jaw to keep from laughing out loud, but he carried on with this charade.

"What's your name?" asked the commander.

"John Doe," said the homeless man.

"Do you agree to never tell anyone that you spoke to Mr. Secret Witness?"

"I swear that I will never tell," said the man. "I'm grateful I was allowed to see you and give you this important evidence concerning espionage." He then handed the small sack to Mr. Secret Witness. When the commander opened the bag, he saw it was filled with coupons: free coffee coupons and two for one deal at downtown restaurants and casinos.

"I'll turn this evidence over to one of our best detectives. Thanks for coming in but realize that you can't see me anymore. This is against department policy. Now, Officer Beal will show you out."

"I understand and I'm glad I was able to help the police," said the mentally challenged man as he waved goodbye.

After the homeless man left the police station, Red stuck his head in the commander's office and commented, "You are crazy! I could hardly keep a straight face. But I guess I should be thankful that the man felt he had his day in court."

"Well it's a damn good thing the bag he handed me wasn't full of shit," said the commander, "or I would have kicked your ass all the way to Fremont Street." Then they both burst into laughter.

CHAPTER 15
Life Moves On

After Red's shooting incident, I would tease him saying, "Honey, I don't think the doctor got all the lead out. Some of it dropped. Now you have some lead in your butt.

Red always referred to the left side as his face as his "John Wayne scar."

When someone asked him what happened, he would say, "I got shot in the head. That's why I act funny." Then he would start twitching his head, scrunching up his face, jerking his shoulders to one side, and squinting his eyes.

People would begin to laugh saying, "You're just pulling my leg." Red would grin back at them knowing for a minute he caught them off guard.

Few people knew that whenever we got a pay raise, we put it all aside. We lived off of our beginning salaries for years. We were very frugal. Every three years we not only had enough saved for trips, but also for a minimum down payment on the purchase of a rental property. First, we bought a duplex, then a triplex. We saved money by doing all the maintenance and yard work ourselves. With all the rent coming in, and only the mortgage payment, taxes and insurance going out, we saved enough to then buy several houses. Of course we had numerous mortgage payments, but our rentals could be vacant one third of the time, and we could still break even. We charged twenty dollars less rent per month than other places in the neighborhood, so we rarely had a vacancy.

Since Red could not go back to patrol, he ran for the position of union president of the Police Protective Association and won. When he negotiated for a new contract, he hired a Certified Public Account, Morton, who once worked locally for different municipalities. "He knows in which areas the money is hidden," said Red. The CPA had been retired for ten years, but still was sharp as a tack. Red wasn't sure if Morton would work for the union, since he had always been on management's side. But Morton agreed and started going over the books like an auditor. He found loopholes. The officers received a nice pay raise that year. The contract was agreed upon by the police commission, because Red had done his homework. He had commitments and handshakes from the majority of the commissioners to vote for the percentage increase. If he didn't have the votes, the negotiations would have continued, even if the old contract had expired. He would then ask for retroactive pay for the officers.

Five years later, Red received a letter from Morton.

Dear Jacob,

I'm writing to ask a favor of you. My health is failing, and I would like you to give the eulogy at my funeral at Temple Beth Shalom. I've listed details of where and when I was born and a brief summary of my life. I would be deeply blessed if you agreed to this. Let me know your decision. Thank you.

Sincerely,
Morton

Two months later, Morton died. We were packed and ready to leave on vacation the day his wife called with the news. Of course, Red would be there to give the eulogy as he had promised. Red never let anyone down. When he gave his word it was his bond. We were the only Gentiles in the temple. I often wondered why Morton chose Red to speak, but I concluded that it was because Red used to stutter, and still does at times. Morton also stuttered and had a speech impediment. Red hated to get up and speak before a crowd, but I must say that I have never heard him speak so eloquently. At times Red could slaughter the English language, but during the eulogy he didn't make any grammatical errors or use the wrong verbs. Morton must have seen something in Red that was a reminder of himself. He must have known that Red would rise to the occasion.

CHAPTER 16
Rowdy Rovers

Red belonged to an ATV (All-Terrain Vehicle) club, consisting chiefly of police officers. It was a wonderful way for these fellows to unwind. They would go to the mountains, either in upstate Nevada, or neighboring states, and ride their quads all day. I don't know if they started out early each morning, but I'm sure they had a big breakfast, before they left for their ride. Eating was a big part of their enjoyment. They cooked outside with cast iron skillets and often layered the skillets three deep. There were a few men who were excellent cooks and took on the job of preparing certain meals for the crew. I called some of their meals, a cardiac by-pass menu, but they were sure good. I knew first hand, because the wives were invited to go once a year on their outings.

The fellows always came prepared, besides food and plenty of libations; they had axes, chain saws, generators, lanterns, and first aid supplies. They were prepared for anything except an extreme medical emergency.

When the guys were on a trip, there was no shaving, bathing or grooming to speak of. One of the rules was that no one could talk about work with one exception: each evening, while they sat around the campfire, they would have "Mad Moment." This was a time when anyone could jump in and cuss about something that had make him angry. After a minute, the guy would have to sit down and forget it. Anyone who complained about the meals had to do the cooking the next day. There were a lot of wild tales, bullshiting, and joking, but most of all, great camaraderie. That was priceless. Red loved this group of guys who were like brothers to him.

On one of the wives' outings, a bunch of us went into town to do some more grocery shopping. The guys knew that I didn't like Red to eat bologna, and I would have a fit, if he bought more than one package per Rowdy Rover trip. It was difficult keeping him healthy. He would put the whole twelve ounces of meat between two pieces of bread, add mayonnaise and cheese, and think he had a gourmet meal.

While shopping that morning, someone slipped a big package of bologna into our shopping cart without me seeing it. When I spotted the meat, I began yelling "Oh no! You don't get any more bologna. "You already had your limit." Red was surprised and denied putting it in the cart. The guys were in the next aisle just laughing their butts off at getting Red in hot water. That tickled them to pieces. When we heard them giggling, we figured out who the culprits were.

Eventually Red had to stop going on the trips, because they were often so far out in the woods, that the cell phone service didn't work. They were far from hospitals or any sort of medical care in the event he had a heart attack. It broke his heart to end the fun of the Rowdy Rover rides, but he had to err on the side of caution.

CHAPTER 17
Burning the Candle at Both Ends

Red was appointed to the Public Employee's Retirement System Board by the governor. I often thought that, if anyone knew that he didn't finish high school, they would be very nervous with him handling a ten-billion-dollar fund. But as anyone drawing their pension will attest to, it has done well, and will continue, because of certain guidelines put in place during his tenure as a lobbyist, including automatic pay raises.

Red was vice president of the Nevada State AFL-CIO. He was involved in local union activities and attended the Democratic conventions. He was also an executive board member of the Southern Nevada Central Labor Council.

As Vice President of the International Union of Police, he went to monthly meeting in Washington D.C., besides winter board meetings and conventions each summer in various parts of the U.S. Sometimes I didn't know what state he was in. I would pick him up at the airport and ask,

"How cold was it in Washington?"

He would say, "Sweet, it was hot in Fort Lauderdale."

"But Honey, I thought you were going there next week."

"No, next week I'll be in Carson City, then Hartford Connecticut the week after that."

He wore so many different hats, I could barely keep up with where he was and which meetings he was attending. I was working one full time job and doing an internship with a psychologist part time, while going to college. We had a large calendar, but there were so many appointments and markings on it, it was nearly impossible to decipher. I tried to attend all the boys sporting events, even if it meant giving up sleep. Red and I were used to getting by on five hours sleep or less.

At age 50, he had his first heart attack. We should have seen it coming. Little did he know that he would be one of the first recipients to receive health care under the "Heart and Lung Bill." He and the Clark County fire chief worked hard to pass a bill in the legislature, that allowed firemen who had lung disease and police who had heart problems, to be covered under worker's compensation, since it was assumed to be job related. One of Red's adversaries said, "Jacob, how did you have a heart attack? I didn't think you had a heart!"

Red answered, "I don't. I gave it to my wife the day we were married."

Often, people would ask me if Red was all right because they saw him with his hand on his heart. I would look around quickly to see if a car or truck had passed by with an Oklahoma license plate. "Oh, he's fine," I would say. "He just saw a license plate from his home state of Oklahoma. He always puts his hand over his heart when that occurs."

CHAPTER 18
Basketball

Red and I enjoyed watching basketball. Season tickets were available to me since I was a UNLV graduate. We were avid supporters of the Running Rebels, and we were fans of Jerry Tarkanian. We managed to go to every game of the season, whether in town or out of town. In 1990, we were in Denver, when we played against Duke and won the national championship.

One day while shopping, I bought a black fleece sweatshirt, that I wore to one of the home games. After two overtimes and cheering until I was hoarse, the Rebels won by two points at the final buzzer. We left the crowded parking lot, relieved the game was over. It was a cold November night, so Red built a fire in the fireplace when we got home. I put a bottle of Bailey's Irish Cream and two glasses on the coffee table. I was feeling amorous. While Red tended to the fire, I stretched out on the sofa in a seductive manner, after removing most of my clothes to entice him. When Red turned around, he burst out laughing hysterically. I thought he was going to split. He would take a deep breath and laugh some more. *Well what tickled his funny bone?* I wondered, as my self-confidence was waning. I glanced down from the glow of the fire and noticed that I was covered with large hunks of black fuzz from my new sweatshirt. There were huge hunks hanging down from my armpits. There was black fuzz on my chest and some stuck in my navel. Yikes! I looked like a hairy gorilla. Well so much for giving the image of being an enticing tart from a *Playboy* centerfold.

At this point I began laughing, too. "Gee Honey, I'm so glad I didn't buy the matching sweat pants. I could have been caged and sent to the zoo." Ever since that night Red had this endearing nickname for me. Whenever he felt like laughing, he would privately call me his "wild thing," just as a little reminder. You could count the times he called me by my real name on one hand. Most of the time he called me "Sweet" or "Ma."

CHAPTER 19
Traits

One quirk that Red had was being on time. He was never late to work, appointments, or flights. I had a hard time convincing him that it was all right to be late for a party. If the get-together started at eight p.m., he wanted to get there at seven p.m. I would say, "No, that's not socially acceptable. We need to be 'fashionably late' because the host won't be ready an hour earlier and may panic. Never be the first one to arrive at a party or the last one to leave," I would caution.

Red was always punctual and had a hard time understanding 'fashionably late.' He would say, "Late is late. Period!"

Another unusual trait about Red was the fact that he liked paying income tax. He was the only person I ever knew who didn't mind paying taxes. He would say, "Just let me have the opportunity to earn the wages, and I'll gladly pay the taxes on it." He didn't mind paying other taxes either. "Without taxes we would never have our roads repaired, wouldn't have public services like firemen and police, street sweepers, etc. We wouldn't have education for the kids. How could anyone fault paying taxes? People use the resources but want a free ride. That's just not how it works! It's like being a non-union worker, a scab. The people benefit in more ways than one, so why should they dodge paying taxes? They are hanging on to the coattails of others who are footing the bill. It's just not right."

Red never gambled or put a nickel in a slot machine. He wanted something for his money spent. He had seen too many people lose their homes and cars. He was one of the few people I knew that didn't know how to play poker. He thought a "full house" meant that you had guests. A "royal flush" meant your toilet worked fine.

He was an avid reader. He read the newspaper each morning front to back. He watched CNN faithfully. Red kept up with the news both locally and nationally. He was literally a news junkie.

He hung the American flag each morning except in strong winds or rain. He was so patriotic.

CHAPTER 20
Travels

While Red was recuperating from his gun shot injury, we decided not to wait until we retired to travel. We started taking one month off each year and go somewhere exotic—Bali, Fiji, Saint Croix, New Zealand. No one can predict what happens as you age. Maybe we would be crippled with arthritis and couldn't get around easily. Worse yet, maybe one would die, and to travel alone would take the joy out of it. We were both working so we set aside money from each paycheck for vacations, plus trying to replace our "rocking chair money."

When Red went to New York for the first time, I was curious to see how he would react. I lived and danced in New York when I was eighteen. I knew that Red would probably be in a state of shock, but that was putting it mildly.

He watched a woman crawl out of a dumpster, hair all matted, wearing only a torn sheer nightgown and eating garbage. Then he saw a man who couldn't leave the curb to cross the street. He would take two steps forward and three steps backwards. Red watched him for at least ten minutes, until I suggested we move on.

Then he saw a homeless man lick his index finger, touch it to a department store show window, then jump back as if it had shocked him. The man repeated it over and over. "What is he doing?" Red asked, curiously.

I just shook my head and shrugged, "*Who knows?*" We then heard cabs honking, followed by squealing tires. Buses and vehicles came to a halt, while an old man ran into the street to play imaginary drums on the asphalt with nothing but a pair of drum sticks. We stopped for lunch, and on our way back the man was still in the street, drumming.

At one point, Red got angry, and quickly pulled me toward the side of the building, when he saw a man on the street corner masturbating in broad open daylight. Red just couldn't believe it.

"Honey, you are in New York City, anything goes. It's the only place a strange person could live and not feel alienated. There's someplace for everyone, and New York is that place. It's also the only place you can find a Lithuanian book store, Mexican jumping beans, a tusk from a mammoth, or anything else you can think of. It's all here. You need not go any farther."

As we headed back to the hotel, Red looked at me so seriously and said, "When I get old and lose my hair, I hope I'm not so vain, that I have to wear a little cap to cover up my bald spot."

"What on earth made you think of that," I said. He nodded toward the man who just walked past us. It was a Jewish man wearing his yamika.

It was fun taking a country boy to the city, but the tables were turned when he took me to the country. Shortly after we were married, we took a trip to Arizona to check on Mom. We went out one evening to a western dancehall. After a while, I excused myself and said, "I'll be back in a minute, I'm going to the restroom." I followed the signs but when I came to the hallway where the restrooms were, I was puzzled by the placards on the doors. They didn't say "Men" or "Women," they didn't even say "Cowboy" or "Cowgirl." I waited for someone to walk out of the door, but no one did.

I went back to Red very frustrated saying, "Honey, What in the heck am I?" He looked at me strangely and said, "What do you mean?"

"Am I a steer or a heifer?" I blurted. He couldn't believe that I didn't know the difference.

"You're a heifer, Honey," he said, laughing.

I guess the funniest thing that I laughed about was when we went to Greece. We arrived at the hotel in Athens. It looked like a palace with its wide marble steps and huge white columns. We took the elevator to the fifth floor, then walked into an elegant room. Red was looking around as I began to unpack. He called out from the bathroom. "Sweet, you have to come in here right away! You just won't believe this!"

As I walked into the marble bathroom, I saw Red sitting on the commode clothed but his cowboy boots were off and his feet were dangling in the bowl next to him. "These Greeks have thought of everything for comfort," he said. "They have a footbath for the weary travelers." "Honey, I hate to disappoint you but that's a bidet." "A what?" he said, puzzled.

"A bidet," I repeated, and it's not for your feet.

I was surprised as we went through the Greek countryside. It was like a time warp. There were bearded men with long hair, wearing white robes, tending their flocks of sheep with a staff. It reminded me of biblical days.

We had loads of laughs riding camels in Egypt. Red flagged down a young camel jockey wearing a New York Yankee's baseball cap, American clothes, talking on a cell phone, and wearing Nike's. "Completely out of character," I said to Red, shaking my head. I waited for an old man in a white robe with the turban around his head and sandals on his feet. Red had bartered to ride for six bucks. I bartered for four dollars, and razed Red about me getting a better deal. I'd hold up four fingers then smile.

I had no idea how tough it was to stay on a camel, but I was soon to find out. The camel kneels, so you can get on the saddle. In order for the camel to get up, he lunges far forward to get his feet underneath him. Here's the zinger. I went head first over the saddle horn, although still holding on for dear life, except my hands were under my crotch. I was looking straight down at the sand from a very high distance. "Holy Shit," I yelled, knowing that if I let go I would break my neck.

The beast then lunged to the right, so he can get his left foot underneath him. Now, I'm lying sideways on the camel, until he lunges to the left, and I'm flipped to the other side. I'm still trying to get my hands out from underneath my crotch, because the saddle horn which I'm holding with a death grip is behind my butt. I thought for a minute that both wrists were broken. I'm all hunched over in an awkward position trying to retrieve my hands. I was wishing I had a seatbelt.

Finally, I was sitting upright and the camel was moving forward. Now I can lift my butt backwards over the saddle horn. I was bracing myself in case the camel hit a sink hole in the sand during my transition. I sure didn't need to slam down on the saddle horn. As I adjusted, we began slowly strolling around the pyramids. I couldn't enjoy the ride, because I'm thinking *how in the hell I'm I going to get down?*

I saw Red's ride coming to an end. My camel jockey took me next to Red, but wouldn't let my camel kneel. He said, "Four bucks to get up. Now four bucks to get down."

"No, No, we made a deal, four bucks for the ride!"

"No, said the camel jockey, four more bucks to get down."

Red was laughing uncontrollably. He held up four fingers mocking me. I was so sure I was getting the best deal but now look at the situation.

"Okay," I said, crossing my hands in front of my chest in defiance. "I'll just stay up here all day, and you won't make any money. Understand?" After ten minutes sitting stubbornly and looking out to the horizon, the camel tender had the beast kneel, and I went through the same upheaval getting off as I did getting on. Red noticed the problem right away. The strap that held the saddle on was extremely loose and badly worn in a few places. It's a wonder it didn't come apart. If it had, I would surely have broken my neck. I could have spent the whole day watching the camel rides. It was the one time in my life that watching, as a spectator, was more fun than being the participant.

In Cairo, where the population was fourteen million, the traffic was horrific. We were in a bus speeding down the freeway, looking out the window, and seeing an old man riding in a cart pulled by oxen, the next lane over, causing a real traffic tie up. Then we really got tickled, when a camel ran along the side of the bus, and looked into the bus window, sticking out his long tongue, and then spitting. Big tractor trailer trucks would whiz by, while pedestrians and children raced across the six lane highway between the traffic. Headlights weren't used at night except, when a car wanted to pass another vehicle. The driver would flash his head lights on, then off. It was pure madness.

Ever since I was a child I dreamed of going to the Holy Land. There was something that always drew my thinking to that part of the world. Red and I went after a legislative session. I called it an "ethnic cleansing," but I had the term all wrong.

I found nothing holy about the area. To make matters worse, when we were in Israel, Prime Minister Rabin was assassinated. Times were tense. Everyone on the street carried weapons including little old ladies on their way to the market. The streets were dirty and littered like in Rome.

We had been sightseeing in Jerusalem until five-thirty p.m. We tried to get a cab back to the hotel. The streets were becoming desolate. When we finally walked inside the hotel, tired from the long walk, we asked where everyone on the streets had gone. "It's Friday, our Sabbath, so everyone must be home or off the streets by sundown," said the hotel manager. We noticed the hotel restaurant was closed, because no one cooks on the Sabbath. We sat in the candlelit bar having wine with peanuts and a bowl of grapes. That was our dinner. When we headed to our room, we found the elevators were shut down. I guess they conserve on electricity on their Sabbath. Thank goodness we only had to walk up three flights of stairs.

During our daily tours the competitiveness was horrible. The Catholics would say, "This is where Jesus was born." The Jewish people would say, "Don't listen to them, Come to see the real place Jesus was born." There would be only twenty-foot difference. Each was fiercely trying to get you to come to their side. I hated the bickering and constant arguing. Our guide was Jewish, very knowledgeable, but extremely rude. He was arrogant and said that the United States didn't give near enough aid to his government. He even cussed at a Catholic nun, when we were at a monastery overlooking the Sea of Galilee. We didn't like that a bit. We reprimanded him and later wrote a letter to the tour company about his deplorable demeanor.

One evening at the hotel restaurant I ordered coffee while waiting for Red to return from the restroom. Meanwhile a large Jewish man sat down next to me and said that I was going to buy him dinner. "No," I said, shaking my head, "you can leave." He picked up the menu and called the waitress over. As he began to order, I said to the waitress, "I don't know this man. He insists that I buy him dinner but I will not and he must leave." The man continued with his order and ignored me. "Leave this minute," I said angrily. He leaned over and spit in my coffee. The waitress disappeared. She had called security.

A few minutes later two young boys about eighteen years old, appeared in dark suits and white shirts. They were small and thin, not weighing over one hundred twenty pounds and didn't appear to be capable of taking on this big belligerent man. They asked him to leave. He refused. The boys then reached behind their suit jackets and pulled out guns, pointing directly at the man's chest. As he stood up to leave, Red returned from the restroom, and saw the young boys pointing a gun at this man, who had been sitting by me. He hurried over to the table in a state of disbelief at what he saw, but, by then, the man was on his way out the door, and the boys were tucking away their weapons. I was glad that it was all over, before Red had a chance to jump in. It would have been an international incident.

But neither Red nor I would ever return to Egypt or Israel, even if someone paid for the trip. There was much deception, too much cheating. Even the bank tried to short change me. There was an unwritten code: if you could get the best of a tourist, you were a better business man. That's just wrong. I had been spit on three times, and not by the camels. We unwillingly had to put up with the rudeness and disrespect. We watched each other's back constantly, being tired and depleted at the end of the day. It was more like a marathon than a month's vacation.

At the airport in Tel Aviv, an Algerian nationalist tried to take my passport but I turned by back quickly, and stuck it in my bra. The authorities were called. He was trying to steal a passport for his wife. He was frisked and security took a weapon off him. He was arrested. There was simply too much tension and strife to tolerate.

We had traveled all through Europe but enjoyed Ireland best. We never laughed so much or so hard. By the end of the day, we were holding our jaws which were sore, from the laughter. In the pubs, everyone seems to join in the fun by playing the spoons, clicking them against their hands and knees. Red has some Irish blood in him, and I am part German and Scotch Irish. The latter is the fun-loving part of me.

Scotland was great, because I took the time to do an ancestry search on the MacGregor Clan. Red thought it was funny that our family name was changed when they came to America, because some of the MacGregors were horse thieves. They were like Robin Hood. They would steal from the rich and give to the poor.

We liked the Scandinavian countries with their many waterfalls. They had interesting folklore telling about the trolls hiding under the bridges.

Russia was beautiful with its winter palaces painted in pastels. Their winters are so severe, that many suffer from depression. The lovely pastel colors gave a cheerful look to the old buildings. The architecture is quite different with the colorful domed roofs. When we were there the economy was bad, and many people were selling their wares on the street corner. Vodka was cheap, two dollars a half gallon. No wonder so many of the older Russians have rosy cheeks.

Africa made us sad, because the people had nothing. Red could relate to some of the third world countries. It reminded him of the poor area where he grew up. It was depressing to him, and he didn't want to ever go back.

In Marrakesh the garbed vendors sitting on their carpets in the middle of the square were hard to see, because it was so crowded. We were walking shoulder to shoulder in the street as the masses moved slowly around. Then someone would trip inadvertently over a vendor on his rug below us. You just couldn't see them. Vendors would tug at the hem of my dress. I didn't want to look down or make eye contact because they were set on selling you something. One man sold teeth from dead people. Yuk! When I stumbled over a basket, I looked down and saw a man with a flute sitting on a small rug. Oh, good Lord, I just knocked over the basket with his cobra in it. I suddenly cringed, grabbed Red by the arm, and begged him to keep an eye out on me. I didn't want to trip anymore. My heart was pounding. Just what I needed, a cobra climbing up my leg, and striking me with its deadly venom. That was enough excitement for me for the day.

We went lots of places, such as alleys in Hong Kong, which were said to be unsafe areas where "fools rush in where angels fear to tread." But we were careful and observant.

Having been police officers we always had each other's back during our travels or in large crowds. It never hurts to have an extra set of eyes looking around to ward off any impending trouble. In the dark shadowy alleys, we found bargains like unframed canvas paintings. They would roll up easily to pack in our suitcase. I never looked for brand name items, because they were usually counterfeit knockoffs. For souvenirs I always bought thimbles which were easy and light as a feather to pack. Red liked to buy sunglasses.

When we were back in the good old USA, Red and I would go to Memphis. We liked Beale Street and would listen to the blues while eating barbequed ribs. After one of many trips to the blues capital of the world, I walked across the street to one of the all-night music stores and bought a harmonica. I serenaded Red all the way home in the RV and promised to learn more songs to play around the campfire. I was really lousy.

Red loved going to New Orleans to pig out on hot spicy Cajun food.

"Honey," I would say, "let's go to the French Quarter so I can buy blackening spices by the case. I also want to look at the colorful, feathered, Mardi Gras masks."

"Sure," he would say, "And I'll buy a Cajun CD." Red loved Cajun music, especially Doug Kershaw. We had been to several of Kershaw's concerts and enjoyed them tremendously. He liked the fast upbeat sounds. Red had always wished he could play the fiddle. I guess that's why he was also a fan of Bluegrass music. There was just something about the fiddle that fascinated him.

CHAPTER 21
Lobbying and the Police Union

Red lobbied in the legislature for the police and public safety. He would say his secret for being such a success was, "Do your homework and count your votes ahead of time." Red was instrumental in getting the Police Officers Bill of Rights passed in 1983.

He was successful in amending the Dodge Bill to enhance the bargaining rights of labor in 1987. When the legislature met, every other year for six months, he would live in Carson City. To save on expenses, he would room with the Clark County fire chief who was also lobbying for public safety. They were a dynamic duo. Red lobbied until he retired from the police department. He made quite a difference for the police officers in the state, and for the retirees with their benefit increases.

Red and the fire chief were successful in replacing private sector members of the Public Employees Retirement System Board of Directors with public employee representatives. This gave them more say on PERS policy. They helped stop the attempts each year by of the lobbyists for the school boards, cities and counties from reducing bargaining powers and rights of the employees. The PERS post-retirement pay increases became mandated by law. Previously pay increases were based on requests at the mercy of the city, county, and state entities.

Years ago, when the union first started operating, Red worked out of the trunk of his car. He handled membership, negotiations, grievances, and started fund raising, so the cops could have a Policeman's Ball each year. He would often hear comments like, "I didn't think cops had balls anymore." Red would just chuckle.

Red could never go anywhere, without running into someone who wanted to file a grievance. We could be having dinner at a nice restaurant, but it usually ended up work related. I couldn't believe that some officers would request union representation, when they were literally caught with their pants down soliciting a prostitute. Red would say, "You want me to waste my time and the union's money by hiring an attorney, when you were wrong and in violation of department policy? My answer is 'No!'"

Nevada Cops, the state organization, would have an annual rodeo each year, which was also a fund raiser. I was always impressed by all the volunteers from the North Las Vegas Police Association and their wives. They handled ticket sales, concessions, the rodeo queen contestants, livestock for the rodeo, and many other odd jobs. They really knew how to pull it all together through teamwork.

The Las Vegas Police Protective Association raised enough money to put a down payment on a building of their own. The offices they didn't need were rented to other police associations. They also applied for a gaming and alcohol license, so they could have a bar. Red's name was on the license, so he had to go before the gaming commission. They always do a background check before approving a license. The members of the commission razzed him about his birthplace asking, "Where is Snow Oklahoma? Is there really such a place?"

Red responded, "You have to go through the town of Ice before you get to Snow. It's in southeast Oklahoma in the heart of America!" He said this with his hand over his heart, and in his Oklahoma drawl. He had lived in Las Vegas since 1960, but never lost his Okie accent.

The name of the bar was the "Debriefing Room", and it was a place where officers could go after work and unwind, not having to worry about a private citizen getting upset, or starting a fight with a cop.

Often after dinner Red would say, "Come on, Sweet, let's go to Dairy Queen." In reality that meant while we were out and around getting ice cream, we would also be checking on the PPA building to make sure the lights were out. Many times, Red would have to go inside to turn off some office lights and turn off the air conditioning units. He was very conscious of the utility bills.

When Red was the vice president of the International Police, he went to Washington D.C. once a month for board meetings. Occasionally I would go with him, because I loved going to the art museums. I always felt bad for Red. As often as he was in D.C., he never had a chance to see any of the Smithsonian Museums or exhibits. He would have loved them, especially the Aeronautical Museum, but work came first for him. We had planned to go back to D.C. after retirement.

One of the last, but very important, pieces of business Red wanted to accomplish before retiring was to pay off the loan on the Police Protective

Association building, which had later been named after him. Looking back, I remember getting a phone call from a woman giving me her condolences on Red's death. I said, "He's not dead. He's sitting across from me at the breakfast nook having a cup of coffee."

"But they named a building after him," she said. "I thought you had to be dead to have something named after you."

"No, Ma'am." I assured her this was not the case.

Red had been retired for several days. He had been waiting for the treasurer of the union to get back from vacation, so he could sign the check to pay off the building loan in full. There was a policy that there must be two signatures (the president and the treasurer) on any check.

Meanwhile, we had a list of things we needed to do upon retiring. Rather than waste time Red began painting the bedroom. He was wearing old torn jeans and a tee shirt full of holes and paint, and an old baseball cap stained from sweat. Right in the midst of refilling the paint pan, he got a call from the secretary of the PPA office.

"The treasurer was just in and signed the check," she said. "You can come down to the office and pick it up." Red put saran wrap around the paint pan and roller and left.

With check in hand he went into the bank, delighted to be paying off the loan, but the security officer thought he was a homeless man just coming inside the bank to cool off on a hot July day. The security guard escorted him out of the building. Red tried to explain that he wasn't a bum. He even showed him the check for one quarter of a million dollars, but the security guard now thought he was, not only homeless, but crazy as well. Red had to call the president of the bank to come out into the parking lot and escort him back inside.

"If I didn't know you, I would have thrown you out myself," said the bank president, laughing.

CHAPTER 22
Senator

One cold January evening we were watching a basketball game on TV when, the phone rang. After the call Red looked at me, strangely.

"What was that about, honey," I said.

"I was just asked to throw my name in the hat for the open Senate seat that will be vacated next week, when the senator from our district resigns to stay in Las Vegas to run for city council. The County Commission will vote on his replacement."

Red had lobbied for twelve years. He not only knew all the legislators, he certainly knew the process. He could jump right in without missing a step. January 1995, Red got the necessary votes to win. He had twenty-four hours to move to Carson City, because the legislature was ready to kick off. We knew that there would be no place to rent, because you would have to start at least six months prior to moving to lease an apartment. So we packed the motorhome, and off we went. There was no problem getting an RV site in January, as cold as it is in Carson City.

There were a lot of things that shocked me. For instance, Red had seventeen thousand constituents, and was given a total of sixty dollars mailing allowance to stay in touch with them. That was for the entire six months. He had been faithfully returning phone calls to concerned citizens in his Las Vegas district only to find out that there was no phone allowance. He had to pay the astronomical bills himself each month. The salary was a joke. Had he not been retired and bringing in a pension, he would have never been able to afford the job. The pay scale was actually ridiculous— $7,800 for two years. When you break that down, it's only $3,900 for a year for all the work involved, and to pay for a second residence. There were additional, utilities, gasoline expenses, dry cleaning, rent, plus all the household expenses and mortgage of the home in Las Vegas. This salary was set by the voters, yet they think that the politicians are overpaid. Not in Nevada. There were many nights Red stayed up late reading drafts for new bills. He literally worked night and day. He had the ability to look at the draft, and immediately pick out the words that would make it too dubious to pass. Sometimes just one word would change the entire meaning of the bill. The drafters of the bill would throw in those words on purpose to confuse the public.

Red liked being a lobbyist better than being a senator. He could get many votes on a bill as a lobbyist, but only had one vote as a senator.

Red never owned a suit other than a Western cut suit with suede elbow patches and lapels. He owned a pair of black Tony Lama boots, and a pair of brown Justin's with tan stitching. He had a tan felt Stetson, which he seldom wore, unless he was outside in the sun. When he was home he often wore bib overalls He really looked the part of the "poor ol' country boy come to town tryin' to make good." Believe me, he was far from a country bumpkin. His thought process baffled me. That's why I majored in psychology. He was my lifetime project.

I viewed things in Carson City, that I didn't want to see. I was reminded of the old saying "When the cat's away the mice will play." I saw married legislators that I knew from Las Vegas, running around and cheating on their spouses, smoking cigars and putting on airs. The position went to their heads. It only fed their insecure egos. They acted immaturely with their newly acquired title's, none of which was impressive to Red or me.

There were several very rich legislators who didn't need to work. They only had the job as a pastime, and to impress others with their title. But the majority were okay, especially the school teachers. They knew what was at stake.

Some legislators wouldn't keep their word or a hand shake. They would turn around on a bill without a call or explanation and vote it down after saying they were for the bill.

There were lobbyists from the National Rifle Association that tried to strong arm Red into voting for the bill on assault rifles. Red being a former cop was adamant about not letting assault rifles on the streets. *How dare they threaten him.* "You are nothing but pimps for the gun manufacturers," he would bluntly say. He shoved them out of his way and kicked them out of the office. It's a wonder he never punched one of them. Red had no patience for people who threatened. His sweet secretary sat there biting her nails, sometimes not knowing what to expect.

Red was outspoken and opinionated. Anyone knowing him would agree. You either liked him or not. There was never any gray area with him. Everything was either black or white. He had been a tough union leader, always standing up for the little guy. Red thought that any hard-working union man had to be a Democrat, although he had a few Republican friends.

The best birthday gift he ever received from me, which he raved about for years, was a card. Inside was a paper from the registrar of voter's office with a change of my political party. Yes, I was once a Republican. Nothing ever made Red happier, than when I changed parties.

For years it had been a hassle during election times, because he would like one candidate, and I didn't. He would have a yard sign for his favorite. I would have a yard sign of the opponent. We had to divide the yard with signs saying "His" and "Hers." Then a string down the middle said "Ours" for the ones we agreed on. If we hadn't done that, people passing by would question, "Why would they have a yard sign for one candidate, and his opponent as well?"

I called our insurance agent to get a policy on Red's mouth. I was afraid that he might get angry and slander someone or hit someone that wouldn't get out of his face. I took out a two-million-dollar policy just to cover all the bases. He had nicknames for certain senators, that he didn't like to be around. The names couldn't be used in public. I didn't want him to slip and be sued.

While in Carson City, Red had joined an old historic organization from the gold rush days called E-Clampus Vitus. I told him the name sounded like some sort of sexually transmitted disease. It was a fun-loving fraternity both charitable and silly. He said it was a good group that helped widows and orphans. Whenever a member said "widder's and orphans" he always chuckled. There was more to their mission statement than meets the eye. They met in what they called the "Hall of Comparative Ovation"—a bar. They really had a flare for the absurd.

One morning a tour was arranged from Carson City to go by bus to a dairy farm to see the operation. Spouses were invited to go. One of the female Senators was wearing all white clothes. I thought, *Who on earth wears white, dressy clothes and white high heels to a farm?* That baffled me.

We first went to the milking barn. The cows were hooked up to the milking machines. One of the rich senators (the one wearing all white) and a freshman legislator got up really close to view the process. One of the cows raised her tail, as I backed up quickly. I'm no country girl but I knew what was coming next. The cow left go. Diarrhea sprayed the two of them, who were up close and personal. They were squirted from head to toe. The expressions on their faces were priceless. It was a look of utter disbelief. I had to run out of the barn because I didn't want to laugh out loud at them. It was all I could do to contain myself. Riding back in the bus was smelly. Every time I looked at Red, he had a smirk on his face. I would have to turn away so I wouldn't start laughing again. They have no idea how many times we joked about that incident. It got a lot of mileage over the years.

Right after the legislature ended we headed to Ohio in the motorhome. We were going to visit my Dad, who was a diehard Republican. Dad had just returned from the local Chili Parlor, where he talked about his son-in-law being a senator. Within several hours, the entire town knew of our pending arrival. We parked the motorhome next to the house and visited inside where it was stifling hot and humid. Dad never had air-conditioning put in the old home place. We didn't want to be rude but we told Dad that we would sleep in the motorhome at night so we could get a decent nights rest.

The next morning there was a weak knock on the motorhome door. There stood eight or nine elementary school kids lined up with pencil and paper in hand. They wanted to know if they could get the senator's autograph. I called out to Red to come to the door. "Honey, there are some sweet kids waiting to see you."

"What do you mean?" He said puzzled.

"Look outside the window, Sweetheart. They want your autograph."

Red stood speechless. That was the first time in his life that he was at a loss for words. He just shook his head, humbly, in disbelief.

CHAPTER 23

Nevada Law Enforcement Officers Memorial

The Nevada Law Enforcement officer's Memorial Commission did a fantastic job of planning, hiring the sculptors, and fund raising for the memorial to be erected on the grounds of the State Capital in Carson City, near the entrance of the Supreme Court Building. A few of the hotels gave generous amounts for this project, but it was also the little donations that mounted up. Everyone's effort paid off.

The life size bronze sculpture on a black granite base depicted an officer kneeling, while cradling a mortally wounded officer in his arms. It represented the Nevada officers killed in the line of duty. Red played a big part in its conception and location. The sculptors needed input half way along with their project. Red asked if I wanted to see the progress of their work, and I jumped at the chance. When we arrived at the home of the couple doing the work, we were led into the dining room, where the model set on a large dining room table. We became very somber and practically tiptoed around the room as if we were at a funeral. The sculptors asked,"

How do you like it?" Our only response was a whispered, "Wonderful." They asked, "Do you have any suggestions or corrections?"

The only question I had was, "Could you add a wedding ring on the wounded officer's finger?"

"Sure, that's an easy fix," was the reply.

On the day of the dedication there was a procession from the far south end of the Las Vegas strip heading to Carson City. As all the police cars headed north, the deputies from the other counties that we were passing through joined the long precession to the capital. It was grand.

The dedication started at noon. There were speeches by various dignitaries. A wreath was placed by the memorial, as taps was played. Good Lord, it was touching. After that the Sierra Highlanders bagpipers, began to play, "Amazing Grace." I couldn't hold back the tears. I wasn't the only one who had tears streaming down my face. So did most of the crowd, especially the families of the fallen officers. It was an emotional day with a candlelight light vigil in the evening. I felt so physically and emotionally weak, I could barely walk. I could just imagine what a drain it was to the families who lost their loved ones.

In May of 2009 there was a Southern Nevada Law Enforcement Memorial erected. It is a regal statue with three tall torches, and midway down an eagle in flight—very impressive. It's surrounded by a lovely park and a memorial wall with inscribed names of some deceased officers.

CHAPTER 24
Family bonding

One year around Christmas time, Red decided to take the boys to Tacoma, Washington to go salmon fishing. A friend had invited them to stay at his home. He also took them out on his boat. They were anticipating the trip, but it ended up a comedy of errors. First it snowed on them while trolling in Puget Sound.

Red was so excited when he yelled, "I've caught one." He felt a tug on his line and reeled it in only to find that he had caught a mallard duck. His friend tried to remove the hook, but it got embedded in his hand. The only thing that Travis caught was a cold. Gregg was the only fortunate one who caught a salmon. We figured that one salmon cost about $1800. Oh well, that was the price of the experience and the bonding.

Another time we decided to give the boys an experience at Mount Charleston Lodge. We took the boys and their wives and children on a sleigh ride through the woods at dusk. This time it started snowing and was most appropriate. The sleigh bells around the neck of the horses rang, as we glided along the path through the glistening snow covered pines. We were all snuggled in warm blankets. It was a magical moment. We ended the evening with cups of hot chocolate at the lodge sitting around the crackling fireplace.

Our youngest granddaughter, April, called her grandpa "Goon Goon." That means "grandfather" in Chinese. Red told her, "It better mean 'grandpa' or someone is in BIG trouble!"

After Red's heart attack, April would say, "Goon Goon had a hard attack." Close, but not exactly accurate.

She was about three years old when she learned the Lord's Prayer, more or less. When she repeated it to Goon Goon, she literally slaughtered it.

"Our fodder who farts in heaven, Hallo-ween thy name." And it went downhill from there.

Our youngest grandson, Zack, would sing with Grandpa Red. Their favorite bluegrass song was "Blue Moon of Kentucky" (keep on shining). Zack was eleven at the time, and their singing was pathetic. Neither one had to worry about anyone breaking down the door to sign a contract for Nashville. They simply weren't ready. But they sure had fun. The more off key they sang, the more they laughed.

We had a couple of wayward grandchildren that lived life on the wild side. We didn't agree with their life style but prayed for them to see the error of their ways and change. A lot of families have to deal with this problem, in one way or another. Often, they turn their lives around for the better.

We went back to Oklahoma for one of Red's family reunions. There was always lots of good food and fun. One year while we were there, we heard there was a homecoming parade and festivities planned in the small town of Antlers, where Red and his sisters had attended high school. They wanted class members to ride on the floats going down Main Street. Red's sister was in the class of 1951, but couldn't ride on the float, because she was suffering badly from shingles. We sat on the sidelines watching. The average age of the alumni from the class of 1951 was 80 years old. Oh, my heavens, I didn't know whether to laugh or cry. Some things get better with age, but not this parade. There was no new blood in town, so the old folks tried to carry on the tradition. In the future, as the class sizes start to dwindle, three or four previous graduating classes will have to decorate and share one float.

Red and I thought that the class of '51 needed to forego the ride down Main Street. Their float looked more like a hospital ward. The only décor was rolls of toilet paper wound around gold garlands. Red and I thought they were trying to portray the golden years. It was pathetic.

A cousin of Red's had a hard time getting on the trailer with his walker not to mention Ida May in her wheelchair. Heck, TJ Burns came right from the nursing home on a gurney and was rolled up on the float by way of a make shift ramp. He had been the grand marshal the prior year and was adamant about participating again. It was hell for Hester who had to be helped down just as the parade started, so she could use the outhouse by the old auction barn. She slipped in cow manure, got it all over the hem of her dress, not fazing her a bit, and was then hoisted back onto the float.

Red nudged me. "Watch who she sits next to," he said, laughing. She took a seat next to Ludlow, who immediately moved away from her as quickly as his age would allow, shouting all kinds of profanity, and shaking his head at her in disgust. He moved to a bale of hay near the front of the trailer but was overcome by the fumes of the tractor's exhaust.

Red commented, "Look at old Willard in the white shirt and the bibs. He's doing the best of all." But then the trailer abruptly hit the cattle guard at the edge of town, and Willard lost his false teeth. He got down on all fours looking until he got a whiff of Hester's skirt hem. He jerked upright like a spry young man.

Mabel took off her sunbonnet and tried to put it on Harvey's head saying, "The sun's reflecting too much off your bald noggin." She didn't succeed.

They all had candy to throw to the onlookers of the parade. Ludlow had all he could take because, Mabel, with her rheumatism, couldn't throw far enough to get it off the float. It kept landing smack in his face "Mabel," he yelled, "Hells Bells, if you can't throw any further than that just sit there and eat the damn stuff!"

Red and I kept thinking that there was barely room for the seven alumni plus their medical equipment. If they had more space, a port-a-potty would have helped Hester. By the end of the parade, there was a little piddle puddle where she sat.

Red thought the class should have been sitting on the sidewalk in their walkers, wheelchairs, or lawn chairs enjoying the parade like the kids and other onlookers, instead of risking any injuries from their participation. But I must admit it was a hoot to watch. We couldn't help but think we were quickly approaching old age, and not looking forward to all the infirmities. I asked Red if we could forego any more homecoming parades. "Yeah, go ahead and call me a party pooper," I said. "Just don't call me Hester."

The festivities weren't over yet. There was a street dance in the evening.

For goodness sakes, there were people coming out of the woodwork, or should I say, woods. Most had no shoes. I gawked in amazement, as the younger generation danced and turned barefooted on the hard asphalt. It didn't seem to phase them. The street had been closed, so the country band could entertain on the flatbed trailer. People stood lined up along the side of the street waiting to be asked to dance. The men would walk up and down eyeing the women. Red nudged me, "Do you feel like you are in a police lineup?"

"You Oklahomans have some strange ways," I said.

Red's sister-in-law turned quickly and headed to the truck. Did she know something, I didn't know?

Oh yes, she did, because a moment later an old bald-headed man was standing in front of me, with a big smile and no teeth. He was a thin man wearing a huge pair of pants with about a fifty-two-inch waist. He didn't have suspenders, so he needed both hands to hold them up. His arms stretched straight out in front of him, so I stepped back because I didn't want to see down his britches. Red looked at me then whispered one of my Dad's famous lines, "Last chance to go steady." I'm not shy or stuck up and I would have danced with anyone except this guy with the trouser situation. If he let go of his pants, they would drop to his ankles. I wondered if he even had on any underwear. I too quickly turned and joined my sister-in-law at the truck. Red shortly followed and said the poor man couldn't get any takers for a dance.

CHAPTER 25
Retirement years

We have been retired for twenty-one years. It's hard to believe that it's been that long. We traveled everywhere we could think of, not only flights abroad, but across the United States in our motorhome. Of course, we would always go to Cancun once a year to refresh and rejuvenate. It was our favorite romantic spot. We would spend two to three delightful weeks in paradise. Years ago, we had searched for paradise, and would fly for eighteen hours to find white sandy beaches, warm beautiful exotic surroundings like Bali. But Cancun was a mere five-hour flight, almost in our own backyard. We had found Mecca.

The only time we slowed down was when we brought my Mom from Arizona to live with us. At first, we hired caretakers to come to the house to look after her, when we took a trip, but none of them would ever return. After that, our sons and daughters-in-law were gracious enough to care for her, when we had a yearning to go somewhere. My Mom lived with us for seven years. It was a challenging experience. We cut way back on our vacations. Mom lived to be ninety-three. Fortunately, we were able to enjoy a few more years of travel after her death.

Red's health was playing havoc with his plans, but he kept on moving forward. He was the cat with nine lives. Much like the old Timex watch commercials, "He could take a licking and keep on ticking." As a cop, he had been run over by a drunk driver while directing traffic on the freeway. He was shot in the head, had two major back surgeries, two heart attacks, four pacemaker/defibulator combinations, prostate cancer, numerous cardio versions and blood transfusions, and that was only half of his health problems.

He became allergic to one of his heart medications. It had built up in his body and poisoned him. But for three weeks the doctors didn't have a clue what was wrong. I was told that it would not be wise to resuscitate him if his heart stopped. "Yes, you will resuscitate him," I said, "because we don't have a diagnosis yet." He nearly died.

At first the doctors thought he had mad cow disease. He was in the hospital for a month, unresponsive and unaware until one day he woke up and said, "I need a shave."

He was back. "Thank you, Lord!" I couldn't resist teasing him about the possible diagnosis of having mad cow disease. His poison symptoms were the same. He took a lot of ribbing from me. No matter how sick Red was, he always bounced back.

At the beginning of the 2013, we got out our calendars to plan our vacation for the year. He wanted to drive the motorhome in the fall to Kentucky to see our older son, and to Kansas to see his niece and other family members. For him to get in the motorhome and go somewhere was heaven.

But he needed more surgery. His hospital stays were getting more often and for a longer period. He didn't like hospitals, and would do his best to show progress, so he could come home. He was a real fighter.

EPILOGUE

Red's last road trip was to his friend's annual "Wild Game Cookout" in Kanab, Utah. That was at the top of his bucket list. I drove him there, and we stayed at a motel and few miles from the function. In the past, we have taken the motorhome, but that was out of the question. He was not physically up to it. Red looked bad and could barely walk but he was so happy to see his old friends. I was glad that we went, because three days later he was in the hospital, again and never came home.

Several of the doctors suggested hospice. When Red heard that statement, he looked over at me and said, "Has it come to that?"

"He's not ready for that, yet" I said. But deep down inside of me, I knew the outcome was not good. True, some days weren't as good as others, but we always took that in stride. We made the best of it. We didn't sweat the small stuff, anymore. But from that time on Red stopped eating and drinking. He didn't open his eyes or talk the last nine days. He was transported to the hospice in hopes of getting him stronger, so I could bring him home. But that was not to be.

I'm not sure he knew where he was. I would put his hearing aids in each morning, hoping and praying that he could hear the boys and me talking to him. At first he would squeeze our hand, but after that he was in another world. I tried to tell him that *he had fought the good fight, he had won the race, he had kept the faith. (2 Timothy 4:7),* but now was the time to concede.

Oh my Lord, I couldn't believe what I was saying. I felt like a traitor. I had always been his advocate, always encouraged him, and nursed him back to health. Now I was telling him to give in.

"It's okay sweetheart. I will be strong. I will miss you terribly, but it's your time to move on and have a big family reunion. No more pain, no more doctor's appointments, no more meds, no more muscle cramps, no more car maintenance, no changing out faucets or repairing the commode, no bills to worry about. You have always valued my judgment, so I am saying that your fight should end. It's time to surrender. God takes over from here.

You have been a wonderful husband and a great provider. We started out with very little, and you made something out of nothing. You wanted to buy rentals, so after our first purchase you kept reinvesting." I thought of the Bible verse. *Well done my good and faithful servant.(Matthew 25:21)* "We have had good fortune and abundance, because God has smiled on us, for which we were always grateful. We have had many wonderful times together and gone places many people have only dreamed of.

Now think of us sky riding in Cancun. Oh, how we loved to go up in the sky in a parachute being pulled by a boat, gliding through the air so peacefully. Remember how quiet and tranquil it was as we soared. It was as though we could reach out and touch God.

Please don't fear this transition. It will be a peaceful one. I don't know if you will be driving the motorhome on the highway to heaven, or if you will be flying there. However, you get there, expect a nice trip. Friends and family will greet you. I love you so much. Thanks for everything you have done. I'll see you later."

He died at four in the morning, I was still holding his hand.

Red wanted to be cremated, and his ashes scattered along old Route 66. As a trucker and an RV traveler, he had driven the route many times. He had always said, "There will be no funeral. When I'm gone, there will be no sad singing and slow walking for me."

In celebration of his life think of him on the Fourth of July. He was very patriotic, so wave your flag. When the fireworks go off, remember how colorful and volatile he was. Light a sparkler and think of him. I know I will.

I felt numb. It was all surreal. I went through my daily routine by rote. I felt empty and had no appetite. I would force myself to find joy in living. I won't sit alone at the long dining room table. I resolved to have friends for dinner often. I remembered what Mom had told me, "In times of grief or turmoil, get busy. Work, work, work." When I couldn't sleep, I started scrubbing the grout in the tile floor with an old toothbrush. If I woke up early, I'd wash the windows of the house, inside and outside, at daybreak.

I cleaned out cupboards and dressers, making numerous trips to the Goodwill thrift store. There is a lot of work yet ahead of me.

"God, I don't know what you have in store for me next but whatever it is I will embrace it. You've been such an awesome God, my comforter and my strength."

"Well, what on earth is this?" Red's alarm clock is sounding. It's three in the morning, and I certainly didn't set his clock. His country's western radio station is blaring loudly. Good heavens, I said as I smiled and looked up.

"Hello Red. It was nice of you to check in on me. It's real comforting."

Three days after that, I walked by his office, and I saw that the lamp by his chair was on. There was no rhyme or reason for this. So again, I smiled and said, "Hello Red. Stop by anytime." Then someone was winding the grandfather clocks, and it wasn't me. No one else was in the house. Saturday was always Red's day to wind the clocks, but they are still running, and the weights haven't moved down one iota. Go figure. I don't mind it a bit. It keeps me wondering what might be next.

Grow old along with me
The best is yet to be…

    Robert Browning

BOOKS WRITTEN BY JORJAN JANE

STIMULUS OVERLOAD

A survival manual for people with Attention Deficit Disorder. It's not your fault. Your brain short circuits and you can't think or focus. Learn how to cope and become the one you always dreamed you can be.

GRANDMA MOONED THE FOREST RANGER, NEVERTHELESS

This is about the difficulties of dealing pleasantly with an aging parent. If you are a care taker, read this. It is mixed with both frustration and humor.

GREGORY

A story of love at first sight. A baby's humble beginnings, written by his mother as a birthday gift to her son. Their trials and tribulations of moving on in life.

TRAVIS

A story written by his Mom as a birthday gift explaining when she first met his dad. Her son's life, loves and pursuit of happiness. An inspiring book to keep moving forward in life no matter what obstacles prevail.

UP BY THE BOOTSTRAPS

A story of a boy from the cotton fields to the oil fields, from a trucker to a pilot, from a cop to a labor leader, from lobbyist to senator. A true story about a boy who picked himself up by the bootstraps, brushed off the Oklahoma dust and showed the world he was someone to reckon with. A story about his life, travels, and success.

www.ingramcontent.com/pod-product-compliance
Lightning Source LLC
Chambersburg PA
CBHW022108050726
47591CB00002B/722